Defending Your Faith

DEFENDING
your
FAITH

AN INTRODUCTION TO APOLOGETICS

R. C. SPROUL

:: CROSSWAY WHEATON, ILLINOIS

Defending Your Faith: An Introduction to Apologetics

Copyright © 2003 by R. C. Sproul

Published by Crossway Books
a publishing ministry of Good News Publishers
1300 Crescent Street
Wheaton, Illinois 60187

Cover design: Chris Gilbert, The DesignWorks Group
www.thedesignworksgroup.com

Cover photo: Ann Cutting/Photonica

First printing, trade paper, 2009

Printed in the United States of America

Unless otherwise indicated, all Scripture quotations are from the ESV® Bible (*The Holy Bible, English Standard Version*®), copyright © 2001 by Crossway Bibles, a publishing ministry of Good News Publishers. Used by permission. All rights reserved.

The Scripture reference marked KJV is from the King James Version of the Bible.

Trade paperback ISBN: 978-1-4335-0315-3

PDF ISBN: 978-1-4335-1157-8

Mobipocket ISBN: 978-1-4335-2259-2

Library of Congress Cataloging-in-Publication Data
Sproul, R. C. (Robert Charles), 1939–
    Defending your faith : an introduction to apologetics / R. C. Sproul.
      p. cm.
    Includes bibliographical references and index.
    ISBN 13: 978-1-58134-519-3
    ISBN 10: 1-58134-519-4
    1. Apologetics. I. Title.
BT1103.S65   2003
239—dc21   2003009625

RRDC   20   19   18   17   16   15   14   13   12   11   10   09
16   15   14   13   12   11   10   9   8   7   6   5   4   3   2

CONTENTS

INTRODUCTION

Years ago I was reading a novel (whose title and author escape my memory) in which a dialogue ensued between a priest and a scientist. The scientist remarked acidly, "You give me your faith, and I will give you my reason." This glib exchange underscores the widespread assumption in our day that reason and faith are incompatible and antithetical. Religion has been banished from the public square (except in times of national crisis) and exiled to a reservation ruled by faith. Faith is viewed as a subjective, emotive quality leaned upon by the weak or uneducated. It is the opiate of the masses, the bromide for the unintelligent. Faith is a crutch to support the psychologically crippled—those who lack the scientific and sophisticated view of the real world.

The task of this book is to set forth, in a brief and nontechnical way, the basic truth claims of Christianity, and to show that at its core Christianity is rational. That which is irrational or absurd is not worthy of either belief or personal commitment. It is the fool who embraces irrationality. To embrace the absurd is to be engaged not in faith but in credulity.

It is one thing to maintain that Christianity is rational, however, and quite another to confuse Christianity with rationalism in any of its many forms. The term *rationalism* comes loaded with much baggage that cannot be borne by orthodox Christianity.

But the problem with rationalism is not reason or rationality. The problem is found in its suffix, the *ism*.

It is one thing to be human, quite another to embrace humanism. It is one thing to be feminine, quite another to embrace feminism. It is one thing to exist, quite another to embrace existentialism. Likewise, one need not be a rationalist to be rational.

An apologist in the twentieth century once observed that the church has become suspicious of reason because she has suffered the "treason of the intellectuals." The loudest guns of criticism fired against historic Christianity have not been salvos launched from *outside* the church but have been vicious attacks from *inside* the church.

Enemies of Christianity have recited the mantra that religion rests on blind faith and not reason for so long that many even within the church have actually come to believe it. This demonstrates the maxim that if you repeat a lie often enough people will begin to believe it.

My hope is that people will begin to see that both rational inquiry and empirical research serve to support the truth claims of Christianity and do not undermine it. I share the biblical conviction that it is the fool who says there is no God (Ps. 14:1; 53:1). The wise of this world are thereby shown not to be so wise after all.

Christianity is based on far *more* than naked human reason but by no means upon *less*. Though divine revelation carries us beyond the limits of rational speculation, it does not sink below the bar of rational intelligibility.

In this book I restrict my concern to the two most crucial issues of apologetics: the existence of God and the authority of the Bible. These are not the most crucial questions of all; the issue of the person and work of Christ is more important ultimately than the question of the authority of the Bible. But from the standpoint of apologetics the strategic priority of the defense of Scripture is clear. If the Bible is established as carrying the weight of divine authority, then its teaching on the person and work of Christ is thereby confirmed.

Defending the faith to the best of our ability is not a luxury or an indulgence in intellectual vanity. It is the task given to each one of us as we bear witness to our faith before the world. I hope this book will help the reader to that end.

—R. C. Sproul
Orlando
Easter, 2003

SECTION I
The Apologetic Task

1

THE TASK OF APOLOGETICS

One major facet of our work at Ligonier Ministries is helping Christians know what they believe and why they believe it. This is the work of apologetics. The task or science of Christian apologetics is primarily concerned with providing an intellectual defense of the truth claims of the faith. The term *apologetics* comes from the Greek word *apologia,* which literally means "a reasoned statement or a verbal defense." To give an apology, then, unlike the more current definition of "I'm sorry," is to defend and argue for a particular point of view.

The work of apologetics rests upon a biblical command. We find a mandate in Scripture to defend the faith, a mandate that every Christian must take seriously. In 1 Peter 3:14b-16, the apostle writes,

> Have no fear of them [those who would harm you], nor be trou-
> bled, but in your hearts regard Christ the Lord as holy, *always
> being prepared to make a defense to anyone who asks you for
> a reason for the hope that is in you;* yet do it with gentleness
> and respect, having a good conscience, so that, when you are
> slandered, those who revile your good behavior in Christ may
> be put to shame (emphasis added).

We are exhorted in this passage to stand ready in case anyone asks us to give a reason for our hope as Christians. This, Peter declares, is one way we regard Jesus as the holy Lord. Secondly,

notice the ethical emphasis in verse 16: we are to answer all inquiries—even the abusive ones—with gentleness and respect, so that
those who revile Christians as evildoers might be ashamed. In this
passage we see the reason for and importance of engaging in the
task of apologetics.

Apologetics in the Early Church

The church fathers knew this task all too well, for the early
Christian community was accused of participating in many devious acts. Leading up to the destruction of Jerusalem in A.D. 70,
Christianity had been viewed by the Roman Empire as a subset or sect of Judaism. But upon the holy city's destruction and
the ensuing Diaspora (scattering of the Jews), the separation
of Christianity from Judaism became evident. The problem for
Christianity was this: Judaism was a legally sanctioned religion in
the Roman Empire; Christianity had no such luxury. The practice
of the Christian faith was illegal and subject to prosecution. The
Christian intellectuals of the time rose up to answer the charges
that were leveled against Christianity.

In many apologetic writings of the period (for example, Justin
Martyr's *Apology* and Athenagoras's *Plea*), we can see four
common accusations against Christians. First, the Christian community was charged with sedition—Christians were regarded as
traitors undermining the authority of the empire. As early as
29 B.C., emperor worship had emerged, most notably in the Asian
city of Pergamum, and it continued well into the second century
A.D. Reciting the phrase *Kaisar kurios* (Caesar is lord), burning
incense to the emperor's image, or swearing by his name was
required in order to prove loyalty to the state. The Christians
refused to grant worship to the emperor and so were seen as
disloyal and as being involved in political conspiracies. While
believing that governments were to be respected (Rom. 13:1-7),
apologists like Justin Martyr argued that Christians were exem-
plary models of civic virtue, paid their taxes, and submitted to the
civil laws, but were unable to confess Caesar as lord because Jesus

was the one and only Lord worthy of worship. Justin therefore challenged the authorities to not convict Christians on the basis of invalidated rumors.

Second, the charge of atheism was leveled against the early church, because of the Christians' refusal to worship the pantheon of Roman gods. Consider the story of Polycarp, Bishop of Smyrna, who, in his late eighties, was brought before the emperor Marcus Aurelius on charges of atheism. The emperor, not wanting to make a martyr out of the venerable bishop, sought to provide an avenue of escape for him. As Polycarp stood in the middle of an arena teeming with Roman citizens, Marcus Aurelius promised to spare his life on one condition: that he deny Christianity by declaring, "Away with the atheists!" The aged bishop, no doubt grinning, pointed up to stands filled with pagans and cried, "Away with the atheists!" The emperor was not amused by Polycarp's gesture and executed him that day as the crowds looked on. Justin Martyr, who was also murdered during Marcus Aurelius's reign, argued in his *Apology* that Christians were not atheists but totally committed theists, who, while affirming the reality of a single, supreme God, denied the polytheism of the Roman pantheon.

The third and fourth charges brought against early Christianity came as a result of rumors concerning their secret meetings in places like the catacombs. From the practice of "love feasts" (where early Christians partook in a common meal—including Holy Communion—attesting to their unity with Christ and each other) came rumors of incest and sexual perversion. The final accusation came from the practice of the Eucharist itself. Early Christians were charged with cannibalism. Word spread that during the secret meetings, these Christians were engaged in the eating and drinking of human flesh and blood. The apologists answered this allegation by explaining the sacrament and calling on the authorities to validate such allegations before persecuting anyone.

In conjunction with these common accusations leveled against the early church, Christians were also regarded as intellectually inferior—often because the doctrine of the Trinity seemed a contradiction to the Greek philosophers. Platonism and Stoicism ruled the day, and most philosophers charged Christians with myth-making. An early glimpse of this collision between the Christian faith and pagan philosophy can be seen in Acts 17, the famed account of the apostle Paul on Mars' hill. Such was the state of defending the faith for the first three centuries of the Christian church. Advocates of Greek philosophy accused Christians of contradiction or challenged the consistency of such doctrines as the Incarnation or the Resurrection. The first defenders of the faith responded ably to these challenges.

In every age the church faces the task of clarifying its truth claims from distortions against these claims. The discipline of apologetics did not die in the second century; rather, it lives on, because with each passing generation, wherever Christianity flourishes, so too do distortion, misrepresentation, overemphasis, and outright malicious deceit. The church's opponents will continue to accuse her of doing evil (this is assumed in 1 Peter 3:16), and so the Christian apologist assumes a defensive posture in order to repel false accusations whenever they come.

The Apologist's Task: Proof and Persuasion

Apologetics, however, does not just entail defense. It also involves offense, the positive task of constructing a case for Christianity that shows itself to be applicable to every culture, as well as being the only (and therefore the best) alternative to the world's philosophical and theological systems of thought. In other words, apologetics can be used to show that Christianity is true and that all non-Christian worldviews are false. The best way to go about constructing a case for the Christian faith is partly the concern of this book. Not all Christians agree on where to start this task. But we do all agree on this: non-Christian thinking, according to Scripture, is "folly" (Ps. 14:1; 1 Cor. 1:18–2:16; 3:18-23).

The skeptic at this point might respond, "Prove it," which is a good thing, because proof is actually another facet of the apologetic task. Sadly, in our day many Christians argue that we ought not to be engaged in attempts to "prove" the truth claims of Christianity, that faith and proof are incompatible. While it is true that Reformed theologians generally believe that human nature is radically corrupt (which is a scriptural viewpoint: see 1 Kings 8:46; Rom. 3:9-23; 7:18; 1 John 1:8-10; cf. John 6:44; Rom. 8:7-8), they wrongly assume that, since in our corrupt nature we are unable to respond positively to the gospel, this spiritual inability renders the apologetic task useless. If objective proof cannot persuade a person to respond to Christ without the intervention of the Holy Spirit, then why bother trying to give sound arguments for Christianity?

Before we answer this objection, let us remember Peter's words, "Yet do it with gentleness and respect, having a good conscience, so that, when you are slandered, those who revile your good behavior in Christ may be put to shame" (1 Pet. 3:16). The apostle clearly expects that one outcome of apologetics is that the enemies of Christ are put to shame. This is reminiscent of the great Genevan reformer John Calvin (1509–1564), who wrote in his *Institutes* regarding the proof of the authenticity of biblical prophecies, "If godly men take these things to heart, they will be abundantly equipped to restrain the barking of ungodly men; for this is proof too clear to be open to any subtle objections."[1] If anyone believed that the total inability of man required the Holy Spirit to convert a soul, it was Calvin. Likewise, if anyone believed in the total inability of apologetics to convert a soul, it was Calvin. He, of course, did not abandon the apologetic task but still used evidence and argument to prove matters of faith—not to convert the hearts of the ungodly, but to "stop their obstreperous mouths."[2] This is a large part of the task of the Christian apologist: to prove the Christian worldview, and to rely on God to cause the acquiescence of the unbelieving heart to the soundness of biblical doctrine. The church is up against not mere ignorance but biased enmity (Rom. 8:7). Only the Spirit can overcome this enmity, but the Spirit never asks people to believe what is absurd or irrational. Calvin noted the distinction between *proof* and *persuasion*. Proof is objective and persuasion is subjective. People who are hostile to certain ideas may have those ideas proven to them, but in their bias they refuse to be persuaded—even by the soundest of arguments.

Apologetics, for this reason, is not merely about winning an argument. It is about winning souls. The old aphorism rings true: "People convinced against their will hold the same opinions still." That is why, for example, if a Christian were to "win" an intellectual debate with a non-Christian, the victory celebration may never take place. The non-Christian might concede defeat, though usually not until his head hits his pillow at the end of the day. This may never translate into conversion, but there is some value to this aspect of "winning" an argument. On the one hand, as Calvin said, the unbridled barking of the ungodly may be restrained; and on the other, the intellectual victory provides assurance and protection to the young Christian who is not yet able to repel the bombardment of criticism from scholars and skeptics. It serves as a confirmation of the Christian's faith.

The Christian bothers to engage in apologetics because, quite simply, how will the nonbeliever hear the truth of Christ Jesus "without someone preaching?" (Rom. 10:14c). Not everyone could accomplish what Justin Martyr or Athenagoras did, but they gave credibility as well as confidence to the whole Christian community of the second century, and by extension the Christian church throughout history has benefited from the fruits of their labor.

The Scope of This Book: God and the Bible

One question we face as Christian apologists is how we should proceed in our argument. I take the position that the best starting point for apologetics is with the existence of God. If we can establish the existence of God first, then all the other issues of apologetics become easier to defend. Others believe that it is better to establish the authority of the Bible first. If the authority of the Bible is established, it clearly affirms the existence of God, the reality of creation, the deity of Christ, and so forth.

Other apologists prefer to argue from history. They first try to prove the deity of Christ and then reason back from Jesus to the existence of God.

In this book, after a discussion of the very important theme of epistemology, which addresses the question of how we can know anything at all, we will consider the issue of the existence of God and then move to the authority of the Bible. I see these as the two macro-issues of Christian apologetics. If God and the Bible (that God is, and that he has revealed himself to us) are established, then all the rest of the issues with respect to Christianity will be vastly simplified. Issues of the Resurrection, the deity of Christ, and so forth, can then be resolved by careful biblical interpretation.

This book, therefore, is both introductory and restrictive. It is not a comprehensive study of apologetics but a primer on the two major propositions we must defend: the existence of God and the authority of the Bible.

2

Apologetics and Saving Faith

If ours is a reasonable faith and not a mere exercise in credulity or superstition, how do we "justify" or prove the truth claims of Christianity? Where does reason fit, in the pilgrimage of faith?

Faith is so central to Christianity that we frequently refer to the Christian religion as the "Christian faith." Within historic Protestantism, faith has also been at the core of the doctrine of salvation. The central maxim of the Reformation was justification by faith alone. With such a strong emphasis on faith, we wonder at what point (if any) reason comes into play.

If one's theology is not merely Protestant or evangelical but more precisely Reformed, the issue of the relationship between faith and reason becomes all the more acute. Reformed thinkers believe that nobody comes to faith in Christ until God the Holy Spirit changes the disposition of his or her soul. All of the arguments and reasoning that we bring to bear in Christian outreach will be to no avail unless or until God the Holy Spirit changes the heart of the hearer. Though apologetics is a task given to us as Christians, and we are to be responsible in the handling of the truth claims of Christianity, apologetics may aid in the planting and watering of the seed, but only God can bring forth the "increase" of faith (1 Cor. 3:6, KJV).

Apologetics and the Three Levels of Faith

Some people believe that since it is the Holy Spirit's task to convert and not *our* task, since conversion is beyond the realm of our power, we don't need to be engaged in a defense of Christianity. They might say, "To give arguments for the truth of Christianity, to give reasons for our faith, would be to undermine the work of God the Holy Spirit." I hear Christians say, "I don't want to study philosophy because I don't want to get in the way of the Holy Spirit."

Though I believe that only the Holy Spirit can change a person's heart and ultimately a person's mind—that only the Spirit can bring a person to repentance—nevertheless apologetics is important in what is sometimes called "pre-evangelism" and also in "post-evangelism."

In pre-evangelism, apologetics supports necessary elements of saving faith. When Luther declared in the sixteenth century that justification is by faith and by faith alone, one of the immediate questions that arose was, "What kind of faith saves?" In words variously attributed to Luther or Calvin, "Justification is by faith alone but not by a faith that is alone." The only kind of faith that saves is what Luther called a *fides viva*—a living faith, a vital faith, a faith that issues forth in works as the fruit of faith. Those works don't count toward justification—only the merit of Christ counts toward that—but without the flowing forth of the fruit of faith, there would be no true faith in the first place.

The thinkers of the sixteenth century distinguished among several actual nuances or levels or elements of faith that together comprise saving faith. The three main levels of faith, they said, were *notitia* (sometimes called the *notei*), *assensus,* and *fiducia.*

Beginning with the third level, *fiducia* is personal trust and reliance, that aspect of faith that involves a genuine affection for Christ that flows out of a new heart and a new mind. It is the *fiducia* level of saving faith that can be engendered only by the work of the Spirit. It is with the first two—*notitia* and *assensus*—that the apologetic task has to do.

The first element of faith is *notitia.* When we say that we are justified by faith, the faith that justifies has to have a *content*. There is certain content, an essential level of information, that is part of Christianity. When the apostles went out to proclaim the gospel of Jesus Christ, they gave a summary of key points about the person of Jesus and about his work—how he was born according to the Scriptures, how he suffered on the cross for our sins and was raised from the dead, and so forth. That is all part of the *notes,* or the data or content of faith. Before we can actually call people to saving faith, we have to give them the information or the content that they're asked to believe, and that involves the mind. It involves communication of information that people can understand.

Before I can call upon Christ as my Savior, I have to understand that I need a savior. I have to understand that I am a sinner. I have to have some understanding of what sin is. I have to understand that God exists. I have to understand that I am estranged from that God, and that I am exposed to that God's judgment. I don't reach out for a savior unless I am first convinced that I need a savior. All of that is *pre-evangelism.* It is involved in the data or the information that a person has to process with his mind before he can either respond to it in faith or reject it in unbelief.

The second element of faith is *assensus.* This is simply the Latin word for intellectual assent. If I ask, "Do you believe that George Washington was the first president of the United States?" what would you say? Yes! That doesn't mean that you have put your personal faith and trust in George Washington. I've just asked you if you believe in George Washington in the sense of whether your mind gives assent to the proposition "George Washington was the first president of the United States."

Sadly, there is a movement in theology today that says faith has nothing to do with propositions—that the Bible is simply a book that bears witness to relationships. It is relationships that count, not propositions. These are the people who think that, "All I need to be a Christian is to have a personal relationship with Jesus. I don't need doctrine. I don't need any theology. I don't need to affirm any creed." "No creed but Christ!" is the call here. "I don't believe in propositions. I believe in Jesus. He's a person, not a proposition."

It is true, as such people say, that one can have a knowledge of the propositions of Christianity and still not know Jesus. We can know *about* Jesus and not have a personal relationship *with* Jesus. Yet when we talk to people about this Jesus, with whom we have a personal relationship, we say things about him. We say, "This Jesus is the eternal Son of God." That is a proposition. The Jesus I want to have a relationship with really is the eternal Son of God. We can't have a saving relationship personally with this Jesus unless we know who this Jesus is, unless we can affirm the truth of this Jesus—that he really did die on the cross in a death that was an atonement, and that it is true that he came out of the tomb. If we say we have a personal relationship with Christ but don't believe in the truth that he was raised from the dead, then we're saying we have a personal relationship with a corpse. That's all the difference in the world from saying you have a personal relationship with the resurrected Christ. All of those things that we say we believe about Jesus involve the mind saying yes to propositions.

If we gain a correct understanding of the content (*notitia*) and assent to its truth (*assensus*), however, this does not add up to saving faith. The devil knows the truth about Christ, yet he hates him. *Notitia* and *assensus* are necessary conditions for saving faith (we can't have saving faith without them), but they are not *sufficient* to save us.

Apologetics serves a vital task at the level of clarifying the content of Christianity and defending its truth. This cannot *cause* saving faith but it has a vital role in supporting the necessary ingredients of saving faith.

Faith Is Not a Blind Leap

Today we have been infected by something called "fideism." Fideism says, "I don't need to have a reason for what I believe. I just close my eyes like tiny Alice and take a deep breath, scrunch up my nose, and if I try hard enough, I can believe and jump into the arms of Jesus. I take a blind leap of faith." The Bible never tells us to take a leap of faith into the darkness and hope that there's somebody out there. The Bible calls us to jump out of the darkness and into the light. That is not a blind leap. The faith that the New Testament calls us to is a faith rooted and grounded in something that God makes clear is the truth.

When Paul encountered the philosophers at Mars' hill, he said, "The times of ignorance God overlooked, but now he commands all people everywhere to repent, because he has fixed a day on which he will judge the world in righteousness by a man whom he has appointed; and of this he has given assurance to all by raising him from the dead" (Acts 17:30-31). This was not a claim to secret knowledge. There is none of that in Christianity. When Paul was before Agrippa he said, in effect, "King Agrippa, these things were not done in a corner. Jesus was crucified openly. Christ came out of the tomb, not in secret, but publicly, where we have eyewitness after eyewitness testimony" (see Acts 26:26).

We may think that Paul's testimony is that of a lunatic and therefore give it no credibility, but we see the difference between making a case for the truth and merely asking people to believe without any reason. The task of apologetics is to show that the evidence that the New Testament calls people to commit their lives to is compelling evidence and worthy of our full commitment. That often involves a lot of work for the apologist. Sometimes we would rather duck the responsibility of doing our homework, of wrestling with the problems and answering the objections, and simply say to people, "Oh, you just have to take it all in faith." That's the ultimate cop-out. That doesn't honor Christ. We honor Christ by setting forth for people the cogency of the truth claims of Scripture, even as God himself does. We must take the trouble to do our work before the Spirit does his work, because the Spirit does not ask people to put their trust and faith and affection in nonsense or absurdity.

The Four Essential Principles of Knowledge

INTRODUCING THE FOUR PRINCIPLES

Epistemology, or the study of how human knowledge is obtained, is indispensable to the apologetic task. As we discussed earlier, one major facet of apologetics is giving an intellectual defense of the truth claims of Christianity. Before we can begin formulating a defense, however, we must first grapple with the questions "How do we know what we know?" and "How can we verify or falsify a coherent apology of the Christian faith?" Christians often respond to these questions with an attempt to offer some basis or ground of knowledge (epistemology). But the varied answers we receive regarding these questions give us a glimpse of the age-old arguments within the study of epistemology. We must affirm a valid epistemological starting point before we undertake an intellectual defense of the Christian faith.

In apologetics, epistemology involves something of an intra-mural debate among Christians. One group might argue that the only adequate apologetic method is one rooted and grounded in historical information, that is, facts known through the five senses. Others contend that the senses can often be mistaken, thereby deceiving those who would rely too heavily upon them. The only method suitable for these people is of the rational or formal sort, such as logical propositions and mathematics. The one emphasizes the senses, the other the mind and the processes of formal reason. Still others argue that the only valid and real way that we can know anything about the Creator is through assuming the triune God at the outset as a necessary presupposition for all knowledge. How to go about establishing a sound defense of Christianity is ardently contested among Christians.

I will come at the question of the basic tools of knowing by asking, What principles are necessary for knowledge to be possible? What assumptions or presuppositions are involved to make intelligible discourse possible?

The Four Principles: Attacked by Atheists, Assumed in Scripture

In the work of the most formidable atheists of Western theoretical thought—John Stuart Mill, Karl Marx, Jean-Paul Sartre, Albert Camus, Walter Kaufmann, and the like—one common theme emerges as they formulated their cases against the existence of God. At some point in their arguments against theism, they attacked one or more of the four basic epistemological premises (all of which are presupposed in Scripture): 1) the law of noncontradiction; 2) the law of causality; 3) the basic (although not perfect) reliability of sense perception; and 4) the analogical use of language. Many of the attempts by atheists to destroy the case for God include a rejection of these foundational laws or grounds of obtaining knowledge. The main reason for my focusing on these nonnegotiable principles is so that Christians may be encouraged not to negotiate them when defending the faith. Rejecting any one of these principles could prove fatal to the believer's case for God. And many Christian apologists are guilty of doing just this.

The Bible makes certain presuppositions or prior assumptions in communicating its truth to those who would listen. Given that the Bible is God's Word, the presuppositions found therein are found in God himself, and are therefore endowed to his creatures, since God has made us reasonable, sensing, and with the ability to communicate. That, of course, is simply another way of saying that God has made us in his image. This is not to say that the

Bible is some sort of technical textbook on epistemology, nor is it a philosophical analysis of how rationality relates to sense perception, or how sense perception relates to the analogical use of language. But we do see, for example, that the Scriptures tacitly assume the validity of the law of noncontradiction, which can be summed up in the following proposition: "*A* cannot be *A* and non-*A* at the same time and in the same sense or relationship." The Bible assumes that truth cannot be contradictory. Consider 1 John 2:22, where we read that anyone who denies the Father and the Son is the antichrist. Clearly, the law of noncontradiction is assumed in this passage: those who say they are for Christ cannot be *for* Christ and *against* Christ at the same time and in the same sense. The Scriptures assume that there is a discernable difference between truth and lie, between righteousness and unrighteousness, between obedience and disobedience. We are therefore held accountable by our Maker. If God commands us to do *A*, then we can know that to do non-*A* would be in direct violation of his command. Indeed, in order to be obedient to God's Word one must assume the law of noncontradiction; the alternative would lead to chaos, as not even one sentence in Scripture could be intelligible without this law.

What about the law of causality? Is that to be found in Scripture as well? Every time a miracle is discussed in the Bible the law of causality, or the proposition that "every effect must have a cause," is assumed. Consider the time when Nicodemus came to Jesus and said, "Rabbi, we know that you are a teacher come from God, for no one can do these signs that you do unless God is with him" (John 3:2). Nicodemus had reasonably connected the dots, as it were, and affirmed the existence of a supernatural, divine cause behind the works of Jesus, otherwise the works could not have been done. The law of causality is everywhere assumed in this statement. If it is not, if we say that anything can cause anything, or that any event can happen without a cause, then no miracle in Scripture—from Creation to the Resurrection—would have evidential value.

Next, we come to the basic reliability of sense perception. This principle affirms the possibility of being deceived by our senses but nonetheless finds our senses to be essentially trustworthy. Surely there are limits to our perception, a fact that the telescope makes clear. But if the senses were basically unreliable, then we could draw no conclusions from what we see, hear, touch, or taste. This would spell the end of the physical and natural sciences; indeed, any knowledge of the external world would elude us if our senses were not basically dependable. The Bible affirms that our senses *are* basically dependable. The apostles John and Peter both attest to having seen the glory of Jesus (John 1:14; 2 Pet. 1:16). Paul, in his first letter to the Corinthian church, says much about the resurrection of Christ and in particular the fact that "he appeared to Cephas, then to the twelve. Then he appeared to more than five hundred brothers at one time" (1 Cor. 15:5-6). If the senses were unreliable, these arguments would be useless. The Resurrection is defended not by inferences drawn from an empty tomb but from eyewitness reports of seeing the risen Jesus.

Finally, there is this arcane idea called "the analogical use of language." The concept simply comes from the word *analogy,* or the notion that two things can be partly alike and partly different. We often point to the similarities between two things in order to describe them and then say that they are "analogous" to one another. The reason why this principle is so crucial is that many theologians and philosophers have argued that God is so entirely different from us that any attempt to speak about him is futile. Because God is so radically transcendent, they say, there is no way to know anything about him, and there is therefore no way to say anything meaningful about him.

Modern philosophers have attacked Christians by asserting that the Christians' statements about God say more about their inner feelings than about anything external. They further argue that the reason talking about God describes our emotions, our religious sentiments, but not an objective reality, is that human language is inherently incapable of rising above the realm of humanity into the realm of divinity. They say that human language is an inadequate tool to describe transcendent reality. Christians are more than able to combat such attacks against the foundations of communication among *humans,* but we must affirm some connection, some point of analogy, between God and us in order to claim that there can be meaningful discourse about him. The key to understanding this concept is found at various places in Scripture, not the least of which is at the beginning: "Then God said, 'Let us make man in our image, after our likeness'" (Gen. 1:26). It is by virtue of God's creating us in his image and likeness that there is an analogy between the Creator and the creature, thus enabling us to speak of God in a meaningful way even within the limits of our finitude.

Our Plan: Four Principles, Five Chapters

It is on these four nonnegotiable foundations that our attention will focus as we labor to establish our epistemological starting point for apologetics. In chapter 4 we will consider in depth the law of noncontradiction. We will pause in chapter 5 to examine the important distinctions among the concepts of contradiction, paradox, and mystery. Then we will resume our discussion with a look at causality (chapter 6), the basic reliability of sense perception (chapter 7), and the analogical use of language as it relates to our ability to know our Creator and respond to him in saving faith (chapter 8).

Again, because atheists have historically challenged these four principles, and because these principles are constantly assumed in the words of Scripture—making them, as we shall see, foundational to human knowledge—we must begin our task of apologetics by showing their validity. If we can do this, then the atheist will be hard-pressed to disprove the existence of God without casting aside one or all of these principles, thereby falling into irrationality.

4

THE LAW OF
NONCONTRADICTION

In 1987, Allan Bloom wrote a book that surprised not a few people (especially those in academia) when it became a runaway bestseller. *The Closing of the American Mind* opens with the following:

> There is one thing a professor can be absolutely certain of: almost every student entering the university believes, or says he believes, that truth is relative. . . . The relativity of truth is not a theoretical insight but a moral postulate, the condition of a free society, or so they see it. . . . Relativism is necessary to openness; and this is the virtue, the only virtue, which all primary education for more than fifty years has dedicated itself to inculcating.[1]

This confirms many other professors' experiences in the classroom for the past several decades. From the cultural revolution of the sixties down to today, gradual changes in the students entering college have been observed, namely, that their assumptions about truth have changed. The student's cry for relativity is indefensible yet nonetheless presumed. Ironically, no one can be a consistent relativist for very long; even when absolute truth is denied to exist, those denying it affirm at least one absolute, namely, that no absolutes exist. In so doing, they assume a rational framework for the world in which they live. Indeed, the assumption of an objectively rational structure of reality is an assumption that is necessary for any obtaining of knowledge to take place.

If truth is relative, then the truth of God is not truth at all but a lie, for the Word of God contends that there is a Truth that transcends the universe, a Truth that is the norm and fountain of all truth.

Also latent in relativism is a denial of logic in general, and of the law of noncontradiction in particular. In the philosopher Aristotle's (c. 384–322 B.C.) own words, the law of noncontradiction states that it is "impossible that contrary attributes should belong at the same time to the same subject."[2] This is equivalent to our own summary of the law above: "*A cannot be A and non-A at the same time and in the same sense.*" Aristotle also articulated other logical principles that we now call "Aristotelian logic." But we must keep in mind that Aristotle did not invent logic; rather he defined it. He argued that logic is a necessary tool for human thinking and communication, as well as a means for us to comprehend the rational structure of the universe. This is especially true for the law of noncontradiction. Denying this law would be like saying, "The book you currently hold in your hands is not a book, but a fish." The law of noncontradiction enables us to argue against such nonsense. Unfortunately, many pseudo-scholars get away with denying the validity of the various laws of logic because they do it boldly, or hide behind arcane philosophical language. But their denials of logic are always *forced* and *temporary*. That is, people deny the validity of this law when it suits them, when they want to avoid a conclusion that logic demands they must embrace (e.g., the existence of God).

On a positive note, when we are engaged in defending the faith, and someone denies this law, the debate is over. Why do I call this a "positive note"? Because if a person claims their disbelief in rationality or logic as a reason for not believing in Christianity, then they have made the case for Christianity. As we defend Christianity we are trying to demonstrate that every alternative to apostolic doctrine is an exercise in irrationality. If the only way one can escape from belief in God is by denying logic, then so be it. .

Noncontradiction vs. Existential Relativism

What makes today's task of Christian apologetics somewhat different, however, is the triumph of relativism not only over the universities but over the Christian community. This did not happen overnight. As a result of the impact of existential philosophy in our institutions of higher learning, many students today go into seminary already convinced that truth can be relative and that the Bible can be contradictory and still be the inspired Word of God. While this way of thinking is astonishing, it is nonetheless pervasive. From the philosophy of Søren Kierkegaard (1813–1855) to the existential theology of Rudolf Bultmann (1884–1976), the Christian faith now carries undue baggage—that of irrationality, which unfortunately translates into the common Christian description of coming to Christ as a "blind leap of faith."

But once again, along with the Preacher in Ecclesiastes, we know that, "What has been is what will be, and what has been done is what will be done, and there is nothing new under the sun" (1:9). As far back as A.D. 200, Tertullian of Carthage (c. 160–225) raised in his book *Heretics* the question, "What hath Jerusalem to do with Athens?" Tertullian wanted to challenge not philosophy generally but something he saw as detrimental to the health of Christian doctrine, namely, the various heresies that arose from Greek philosophy. He was basically wondering (somewhat skeptically) what the Bride of Jesus Christ had to do with the Mecca of secular philosophy. Ever since Christians began using language borrowed from "Aristotelian logic" there have been those who argue that Christianity is no place for Greek philosophy to intrude. Surely no Christian would disagree with this if such philosophy were to give rise to heresy. But we must remember that Aristotle did not *invent* logic any more than Columbus invented

America. All that Aristotle did was discover and define rules that
were already in existence. Aristotle ascertained the necessary conditions for human beings to carry on meaningful conversations.
He defined the proper relationships of propositions. He did not
create the laws of logic; he merely articulated what was already
there. These laws were placed in our minds by the Creator during
the act of creation. We speak because God has spoken. God is not
the author of confusion, irrationality, or the absurd. Furthermore,
his words are meant to be understood by his creatures, and a necessary condition for his creature's understanding of those words
is that they are intelligible and not irrational.

Is Contradiction a "Hallmark of Faith"?

Existential philosophy has had quite an impact upon the church.
One such impact came from the immensely influential Swiss theologian Emil Brunner (1889–1966). In his famous book *Truth as
Encounter,* Brunner wrote that contradiction is the hallmark of
truth. That idea blazed through the theological world and was
well received for a time. It suggests not only that contradictions
are permissible but that we may embrace them and indeed glory
in them, because they are the very hallmarks of truth. Suppose,
however, that we applied this principle to the Scriptures.

In Genesis 2, God spoke to Adam and Eve in the garden and
set forth one major sanction: "You may surely eat of every tree
of the garden, but of the tree of the knowledge of good and evil
you shall not eat, for *in the day that you eat of it you shall surely
die*" (vv. 16-17, emphasis added). If we were to translate this
into logical propositions it might read like this: "If you eat (*A*),
then you die (*B*)." Then the serpent sidles up to Eve in the following chapter, and after a few seductive, somewhat crafty inquiries
about God's command, the serpent flatly contradicts what the
Creator has spoken: "You will not surely die. . . . and you will
be like God" (3:4-5). Again, in logical terms, this looks like the
following: "If you eat (*A*), then you will *not* die (non-*B*)." We
can see that the law of noncontradiction is everywhere assumed

at this point. Adam and Eve saw the contradiction and chose to eat the fruit anyway. But what if our first parents had applied Brunner's theology to the situation? Adam and Eve's thoughts might have gone as follows: "I learned from an astute fellow that contradiction is the hallmark of truth. Since the serpent in this case is the one who speaks the contradiction, he must therefore be an ambassador of truth, and therefore a representative of God. In order for us to embrace the truth and fulfill our roles, we not only may eat from the tree, but we *must* eat from it to be obedient to God." The reader can see how this principle reduces to the absurd. If contradiction is a hallmark of truth, then there is no way we can differentiate between right and wrong, good and evil, obedience and disobedience. Such disregard for absolute truth cannot help but undermine the veracity of God's Word.

One final word about the law of noncontradiction: it tells us nothing by itself. The law of noncontradiction has no content. That is, this and other logical laws do not tell us *what* to think but *how* to think. They are tools with which we can, for example, determine the relationship between two statements to see whether they are contradictory, or whether a person's conclusions validly follow from his or her premises.

The classic syllogism "All men are mortal; Socrates is a man; therefore Socrates is mortal" should help us better understand this point. First, we see that there are propositions here that, if we look at them logically, relate in some way. Logic tells us how to find the conclusion beyond all shadow of doubt. *If* all men are mortal, and *if* Socrates is a man, then what is Socrates? He is undoubtedly mortal. So, then, the truth of the conclusion is determined by the validity of the argument, and logic provides the necessary tools with which we can examine the relationship between the premises and the conclusion. God has endowed his rational creatures with logic so that they might recognize the coherence of his revelation over against the inherent chaos of any worldview that denies him.

God has divinely revealed himself in his Word, not through

the absurd, but through order and coherency. While we should never presume to know the content of God's Word exhaustively, we should also never assume that he calls us to embrace irrational contradictions as a means to trust in him. Far from this is the Logos, the Word made flesh, who is "the true light, which enlightens everyone" (John 1:9). By virtue of God's endowing us with reasoning similar to his own, we can and should expect him to have spoken intelligibly and coherently to his creatures.

5

CONTRADICTION, PARADOX, AND MYSTERY

As we explore the importance of the law of noncontradiction further we must be careful to distinguish it from closely related notions that are often confused with the notion of contradiction. Three important English terms often wrongly used as synonyms are *contradiction, paradox,* and *mystery.* While these three words are closely related, they must nonetheless be distinguished from one another.

In a recent journal article, a scholar argued against Christian theism and ridiculed it, writing that at the heart of historic Christian orthodoxy is the doctrine of the Trinity, a doctrine that no rational person could embrace because it is absurd. He made this charge because he was convinced that the doctrine of the Trinity violates the law of noncontradiction, thereby violating logic itself. This accusation against the doctrine of the Trinity should come as no surprise; many individuals argue in this fashion. What is surprising, however, was that this assault was leveled by a professor of philosophy—a professor who should have known the law of non-contradiction well enough to realize that the doctrine of Trinity does not in fact violate this logical principle.

Contradiction vs. Paradox

The historic doctrine of the Trinity asserts that God is one in essence, or substance, and three in person. If we write this in logical terms it would look like the following: God is one in *A* (essence), and three in *B* (person). According to this principle, we see that the Trinity does not violate logic. Orthodoxy asserts that God, with respect to one thing, is unified, but with respect to another he has diversity or plurality. God is three in one thing, and one in another thing. This is no contradiction. A contradiction would occur if we said that God was one in essence (*A*) and three in essence (non-*A*), or three in person (*B*) and one in person (non-*B*), in the same sense and at the same time.

What we have with the doctrine of the Trinity is not a violation of the law of noncontradiction but a *paradox*. Linguistically, the word *paradox* comes from the Greek words *para* (that which is alongside something else) and *dokeo* (seem). The word *paradox* simply describes a statement that, while true, has an *appearance* of contradiction. The word was important during the first few centuries of the Christian church. As the Trinitarian debates raged, Docetism (also from the Greek word *dokeo*) argued that Jesus "seemed" or "appeared" to have a human body and to be a human person, but his body was only a phantom. Docetism was a subset of Gnosticism. Gnostics, generally speaking, disdained materiality and the physical as inherently evil. This thinking fell in line with ancient Greek philosophy, which held that if anything spiritual were ever brought into contact with the physical, then the spiritual would become contaminated because flesh was, by nature, imperfect and corrupt. One can see, then, how the great stumbling block for the Gnostics was not so much the resurrection of Jesus but his incarnation. The notion of a spiritual God taking upon himself a human nature and body repulsed them. The Docetists in the early church argued from these premises that Jesus was really a "phantom," that he only appeared to have a human body. (As an aside, how does the apostle John handle such thinking in his first epistle? "By this you know the Spirit of God: every spirit that confesses that Jesus Christ has come in the flesh is from God, and every spirit that does not confess Jesus is not from God. This is the spirit of the antichrist" [1 John

4:2-3]. This theory of the docetic [phantom] Christ that denied the reality of his physical body was considered by John, and by extension the New Testament writers, to be not just heretical but of the same spirit as the antichrist.)

The Gnostics failed to examine the Incarnation more deeply. The Incarnation, at first glance, may seem contradictory, but upon a closer look we see that in fact the Incarnation, like the Trinity, is no contradiction at all. The orthodox Christian church did not confess that Jesus is God (*A*) and not God (non-*A*), or man (*B*) and not-man (non-*B*). Rather, the church declared that Jesus is both *truly* God (*A*) and *truly* man (*B*). He is both *A* and *B,* with all of their respective attributes. God is one in nature (essence) and three in person. Christ is one in person, but two in nature. Neither of these formulae is contradictory, but both are paradoxical. The Holy Scriptures are filled with such paradoxes, especially in the teachings of Jesus. Consider Matthew 10:39, where the apostle records Jesus saying, "Whoever finds his life will lose it, and whoever loses his life for my sake will find it." Is this contradiction or paradox? If Jesus were calling his hearers to lose their lives at the same time and in the same way that they find their lives, then he would be speaking nonsense—pure contradiction. But if he meant that in one sense they must lose their lives in order to find their lives in another sense, then this statement is a paradox—at first glance, a seeming contradiction, but at second glance, a profound truth.

Contradiction, Paradox, and Antinomy

The distinction between contradiction and paradox is a clean distinction. If we understand the difference between the two words, we shouldn't stumble into the difficulties that many people stumble into. Unfortunately, there's another term that tends to muddy the waters, and that's the word *antinomy*.

In classical philosophy, the term *antinomy* is equivalent to the word *contradiction*. That is, in classical philosophy, an antinomy is a contradiction.

Contradiction comes from the Latin. "Contra" is the prefix, which means "against"; literally, a contradiction is speaking against something. This becomes even more clear when we analyze the word *antinomy,* which comes from the Greek. "Anti" is the prefix, which means "against," and the root is the Greek word *nomos,* which means "law." An antinomy literally is *against law.* The law that is in view, in the origin of this word, is the law of noncontradiction. An antinomy is a violation of the law of noncontradiction and therefore is a contradiction. Both of these terms, *contradiction* and *antinomy,* historically and classically mean the same thing. Unfortunately in our day, they are used differently, and often *antinomy* will be used as a substitute or an equivalent for *paradox.*

If we were to go to some recent editions of English dictionaries, we would see *antinomy* and *paradox* given as synonyms for *contradiction.* How do we explain that? Language is fluid. It undergoes certain changes over time. When a lexicographer sets about the task of defining words and preparing a dictionary, he studies the "etymology" of the word, which involves at least three major considerations. First, he looks at the origins of the word. In the case of "contradiction," he would go back to the original Latin; in the case of "antinomy," he would go back to the Greek. Then he looks at the historical usage. If we look at the multivolume set of the *Oxford English Dictionary,* we see references to how words were used historically. There may be citations, for example, from Shakespeare, showing how Shakespeare, in his age, used a particular term, and then bringing it down through the centuries, showing how the word undergoes subtle shifts in nuance. But the final criterion by which lexicographers define words is *contemporary usage.* They keep their ear to the ground and see how modern people are using the term. If enough people use a word incorrectly, and they do it often enough, that formerly incorrect use of the term will become its correct meaning. I am not at all surprised, then, to see some modern dictionaries calling *paradox* and *antinomy* synonyms for *contradiction,* even though historically there are crucial distinctions among them.

However, since we are talking philosophically and theologically, I am using these terms in their historical sense, not in the way in which they are muddled together in our contemporary culture.

Mystery

If confusion exists among these terms, the confusion becomes even greater when we add the next category into the mix—the category of *mystery*.

When we affirm the doctrine of the Trinity, even though we can define what it is not (i.e., it is not a contradiction), we are nonetheless unable to penetrate the depths of what it actually is. In like manner, at the Council of Chalcedon in 451 the church put a fence around the doctrine of the Incarnation. The Council affirmed that Jesus is truly God and truly man, and that these two natures are distinct but perfectly united; they are not confused, mixed, separated, or divided. The church did not, however, presume to define exhaustively *how* the union of Jesus' two natures exists; it just built a virtual arena in which the orthodox could function. What remains, what the church did not articulate, is *mystery*. No one can describe exactly what took place when the Word became flesh. We do not know how the divine nature and the human nature coexist in the Incarnation. That remains a mystery to us. An exhaustive knowledge of God is beyond us. Being finite, we cannot exhaustively grasp the infinite.

It is important to understand, however, that the fact that something is mysterious does not invalidate its truthfulness. If such were the case, the study of science itself would collapse. There is still much to learn in various fields such as science, mathematics, social studies, and theology. While some things are more mysterious to one person and less so to another, no one, save God, has exhaustive knowledge of the past, present, and future. When dealing with an electrical problem, one person may be mystified about anything beyond checking the light bulb and fuse box. To an electrician, however, there is much less mystery. The same applies to Christianity. People may find all sorts of mysteries within the Christian faith, but there are theologians who have studied and unraveled what are mysteries for others. Theologians, of course, never fully understand the things of God. They may find that the unraveling of one mystery opens the door to several more, proving the adage that the more we learn, the more we realize how little we know.

Mystery vs. Contradiction

Mystery involves a lack of understanding or an absence of knowledge. If there is any point of contact between contradiction and mystery, it is this: both contradictions and mysteries are not understood *at present*. But one important difference remains: contradictions can *never* be understood—they are inherently unintelligible. Even God cannot understand a contradiction. For God there is no such thing as a square circle. However, in time, with the gaining of more information, what is a mystery *now* may be revealed. The statement "The book in your hand is not a book" will never make any sense. But that same book in a baby's hand, though unintelligible at the time, will not remain a mystery for very long. Mystery is a legitimate element of reality, a legitimate part of pursuing knowledge, and should provoke a response of humility within us. But mystery cannot and must not be used as a license to embrace contradiction. This happens repeatedly, especially in our current relativistic culture. People (even philosophy professors) improperly assume things are contradictions and think that if they attain more information they will be able to unwrap the contradiction. But a contradiction by its very nature can never be understood; even with all the knowledge in the world or an eternity of examination, a bona fide contradiction will always remain unknowable. These crucial differences among the categories of mystery, paradox, and contradiction must not be underestimated. Contradictions came from the serpent's mouth in the garden, while paradoxes show us the profoundest of truths, and mysteries lead us to cry with Paul, "Oh, the depth of the riches and wisdom and knowledge of

God! How unsearchable are his judgments and how inscrutable his ways!" (Rom. 11:33).

Perhaps the greatest danger we face in theology today involves the confusion of these distinct categories. We have theologians who do not blush at affirming both poles of a contradiction. I had a seminary professor who once declared, "God is absolutely immutable in his essence," and, "God is absolutely mutable in his essence." He said this with furrowed brow and in hushed tones as if he were uttering a profundity. The students were duly impressed, thinking, "Wow! That's really deep." In fact his assertion was not profound: it was profoundly absurd.

Today within evangelicalism there is a new epidemic spread by thinkers who argue that since God is a higher order of being from us, real contradictions may be resolved in his mind—that God is not bound by the human rules of logic. Such a view sounds pious, but it effectively undermines the entire biblical revelation. If contradictions can be reconciled in the mind of God, then we cannot trust a word of Scripture, for in God's mind Christ might also be antichrist.

Mystery? Yes. Contradiction? No. We must be careful to observe the difference.

6

THE LAW OF CAUSALITY

As we continue our examination of the four nonnegotiable principles of knowledge, we will now consider the law of causality. This law, as we shall see, is actually only an extension of the first principle, the law of noncontradiction. The law of causality is necessary for the acquiring of knowledge, and has been assumed by all people since the beginning of human existence. Causal thinking is especially important to the natural sciences. Likewise, the sacred Scripture assumes the law of causality and frequently appeals to causal connections. To reject any of the four principles, including causality, hurls us into chaos, making knowledge about the external world impossible.

As we have seen, however, many people—especially the opponents of Christianity—do reject these principles. Since these four principles provide a solid foundation upon which the Christian can soundly defend the existence of God, we should expect those who deny the existence of the biblical God to attack this foundation by attacking these principles. What better way is there to escape the demands of a holy God than to deny the fact that humans can know anything about him? Christians rightly affirm, however, that refusing the knowledge of God only leads to folly (Ps. 14:1; cf. Romans 1).

The law of causality has enjoyed great respect throughout the history of Western theoretical thought and has been a formidable argument for the existence of God. By reasoning from the appearance of this world (i.e., as one large effect) back to an adequate or sufficient cause, both Christians and people of other religious faiths seek to show the extreme plausibility that the very first cause is God. This "cosmological proof" has been in use for millennia, finding its roots in Aristotle, who argued that the existence of a supreme being was necessary simply because events require a cause, and there needs to be an uncaused (or first) cause in order to make sense of the world.

Causality Under Attack

Since the eighteenth-century Enlightenment, however, the law of causality has undergone much criticism by skeptics (those who maintain that knowledge of universal truths cannot be attained). Bertrand Russell (1872–1970), for example, in his book *Why I Am Not a Christian,* gives a personal testimony about his pilgrimage regarding theism. Recounting his childhood, Russell writes that he was deeply impressed with the argument for God's existence from the law of causality—until he encountered John Stuart Mill. Mill (1806–1873), a London-born philosopher belonging to the school of what is now called "utilitarianism" or "consequentialism," once wrote an essay called "Theism" in which he rejected causal thinking. He argued that nature had in itself a permanent, uncaused element: "as far as anything can be concluded from human experience, Force has all the attributes of a thing eternal and uncreated."[1] This belief basically drove Mill to write that "if everything must have a cause, then God must have a cause."[2] When Bertrand Russell read this essay at age seventeen, he described it as an epiphany: he came to the conclusion that the law of causality would not lead to the first cause (God) but only to an endless regression that yields nothing.[3] To Russell's mind, arguing for the existence of God on the basis of causality commits an egregious fallacy.

Simply put, this was one of those enigmatic moments where brilliance meets dullness. While Mill was unarguably a fine philosopher, well-trained in logic and skilled in analytical thought, he made a fundamental error in his definition of causality. He assumed that the law of causality is simply, "Everything must have a cause." If indeed the law could be defined in this way, then Mill's criticism would be just. But such is not the case. The law of causality does not require that *everything* have a cause, only that every *effect* must have a cause. An eternal object need not have a cause—Aristotle got that right. If Mill would have gotten it right, perhaps Russell would not have been led so far astray. What we must strive to do, then, is find something that is not an effect, something that has the power of being within itself, something that has existed from all eternity. (It might be obvious to the Christian that this "something" is God, whom orthodox Christians have historically described as self-existing, eternal, and independent of all things. He is not caused simply because he is not an effect.)

Causality: True by Definition

The simple definition "every effect must have a cause" is a "formal" or "analytical" truth. When a statement is analytically true it means that it is true by definition—that if one analyzes the words within the statement and their relationship to each other, then it is clear that by its very definition, it has to be true. For example, the statement "All bachelors are unmarried men" is necessarily true just as "Some bachelors are married men" is necessarily false. What makes these statements analytic and therefore true is that they contain in the words themselves all that is needed to recognize their truth. That is, "bachelors" are "unmarried" *by definition*. Nothing else is required for us to know this than what is already present in the statement, "All bachelors are unmarried men." The same applies to the following: "A triangle has three sides." This is true not only because we see that triangles do indeed have three sides but because triangles, *by definition*, are three-sided figures. The law of causality is just as logically true as are these analytic statements.

Looking more closely at the definition of this law ("every

effect must have a cause"), how are we to define "effect"? Does
it not carry with it an obvious definition? An effect is "that which
has been caused." An effect, by definition, is something that has
been caused by something else. The word "cause" is also self-
evidently defined, for it, by definition, brings about some kind of
a result, or "effect." A cause cannot be a cause unless it produces
an effect. We cannot have a cause without an effect. Thus, "All
causes have effects and all effects have causes" is an analytic statement and must be true. If something can be shown to be an effect,
then as an effect it requires a cause. This shows us more clearly
how the law of causality ("every effect must have a cause") is
really an extension of the law of noncontradiction. That is, an
event (A) cannot be an effect (B) and fail to be an effect (non-B)
at the same time and in the same relationship. The same applies
to the idea of "cause"; otherwise, a clear contradiction would
emerge, making knowledge of ourselves and the world impossible (because, the reader will recall, contradictions are eternally
unknowable).

As with all logical propositions, the law of causality does not
impart information to us about reality, nor does it prove that
both causes and effects even exist in the world. But the law does
show us this: *if* many objects exist in the world, and *if* any of the
objects can be defined as an effect, then we can know for certain
that the world has a cause. Maybe the many objects that fill the
world are not effects, but that is not the point. The logical principle of cause and effect simply dictates that *if* something can be
established as an *effect,* then the necessity of a cause has at the
same time been established. As an example of the force of this
universal truth, consider the following account.

Several years ago, I coauthored a book on classical apologetics. While reading a critique of the book by a well-known philosopher, I came across a statement I will never forget. "The problem
with Sproul and his book," he wrote, "is that he will not allow for
an uncaused effect." Now, as a basic rule, I never engage review-
ers in debate or discussion. After all, it is their job to criticize. But

this particular comment I could not let go. I wrote a short letter to the philosopher that said something to this effect:

> You wrote in your review that one major problem with my book was that I would not allow for an uncaused effect. *Mea culpa.* You are absolutely right. But I thought my adamant refusal to not allow for uncaused effects was a virtue—not a vice. However, I would be most happy to recant if you would take the trouble to write me at least one example, anywhere in the entire universe, of an uncaused effect.

I am, of course, still awaiting his response. I gather that he realized, upon a moment's reflection, that it is quite impossible to have an uncaused effect, because an effect, by definition, is something that has a cause.

The misconstrued definition of the law of causality ("*everything* must have a cause" rather than the correct "every *effect* must have a cause") is only one reason why so much doubt has been leveled against this law. The other reason, which we will explore in the next chapter, comes by way of David Hume's (1711–1776) watershed critique of causality. Almost every philosopher since Hume who has rejected causal thinking has believed that the British empiricist philosopher actually demolished causality. But that is far from the truth, as we will demonstrate. Once again, if the power of causal thought drives people to acknowledge a sufficient cause (e.g., God) for the things that we recognize as effects (e.g., the world), then what unregenerate person would want to embrace the law of causality? In essence, such people want to avoid acknowledging their Creator, for, as we learn from Romans 1, acknowledging God is tantamount to giving thanks to him, and giving thanks to him is tantamount to loving obligation and self-denial.

7

HUME'S CRITIQUE OF CAUSALITY
AND THE BASIC RELIABILITY OF
SENSE PERCEPTION

The unregenerate person, as we have learned in the writings of Paul, will believe anything about God except that which has been clearly revealed in the Scriptures or in creation (Rom. 1:18ff; 8:7). This is why many nonbelieving empiricists presume that David Hume's critique demolished the law of causality. Although Hume is usually accused of doubting causal relations (that there is ever a necessary connection between an effect and a cause), he actually argued that the real problem with causal relationships is that we cannot determine precisely the particular cause of a particular effect. He sought to demonstrate that we never are able to *perceive* causality at work.

Again, Hume did not destroy a pivotal principle like the law of causality; he did argue that we cannot really trust causal relationships to explain certain aspects of reality (such as the existence of God).

Those who have come after Hume, however, whose atheistic desires have been to show that God does not exist, use Hume's critique (wrongly) to prove their case. Contrary to popular opinion, however, Hume did not demolish the law of causality. What he said was that when we observe events around us that follow one another in time, we assume that the previous event actually caused the subsequent event. Since we observe this on a regular basis, we assume that these events are always caused by what preceded them. Hume called these "customary" or "contiguous" relationships (i.e., things that are adjacent to each other are "contiguous" to one another). For example, when it rains, the grass becomes wet. Given that we observe this happening every time it rains, we reach the conclusion that the *cause* of the wet grass is the rain. In Hume's terms, the rain is "contiguous" to the wet grass—they share a customary relationship because the event of wet grass follows the event of rain. So, we assume cause (rain) and effect (wet grass) as a way to make sense of the world in which we live.

No Cause? Or No Ability to Know the Cause?

All of this surely seems preposterous to the observant reader. Why make an argument about whether the rain is the cause of the wet grass? During the early modern era, philosophical wars were being waged about the existence and location of causes. The Rationalists (Descartes, Spinoza, Leibniz) all postulated (in different degrees) that the actual causes may in fact be invisible, that is, not observable through the senses. But what concerned Hume was not doubting the existence of actual causes (that some things can and do cause changes in other things), but how we come to *know* causal relationships.

By way of illustration, with the invention of the microscope came a whole new world of invisible (to our eyes) organisms that we now know to be causes of various infections and diseases. Prior to this discovery, many people were blaming sicknesses on evil spirits, too much of one bodily fluid over another, and so forth. In the same way, Hume argued that there are many events we do not perceive with our senses, and that we make assumptions about the events we do see, namely, that just because one thing follows another, the first must therefore be the cause of the second. Consider another illustration, this time from Hume himself.[1] In his analysis of causality, Hume instructs the reader to imagine a pool table with a pocket at the opposite end of the table from a pool player holding a cue. On the table, in front of the player, is the cue ball. Beyond a stretch of green, in the center of the table, lies the object ball (hereafter called the "eight ball"). Imagine that the pool player desires to sink the eight ball into the pocket. Assuming he or she knows the rules of the game, the player chalks the end of the cue and aims it at the cue ball. Using the conventional technique, the player's arm swings, striking the ball with the cue, presumably imparting the necessary force to set the ball in motion. Assuming the player's accuracy, the cue ball then moves across the table and hits the eight ball, which, also assuming the player's accuracy, then moves in the direction of the pocket and ultimately falls inside. As we can see, many physical events have transpired in order for the eight ball to sink into the pocket. From the player, to the cue, to the swinging motion—all of these serve to reinforce the notion that there is a causal relationship between the player and the sinking of the eight ball. But how can this causality be perceived? Can we actually see the force coming off the cue when it strikes the cue ball? Obviously not. What we do see, Hume argued, is a customary ("contiguous") relationship—one event following another. Hume was attempting to show that we cannot use reason or the senses to perceive causality, that we cannot actually see causal relationships, only events that transpire in a sequence. All references to causality, then, or "first causes," are merely assumptions based on our observations of customary relationships. And this is the heart of the matter for Hume: since we cannot truly know causality by way of reason or our senses, and since there is no other way than reason or our senses to know anything at all, causality can never be known with precision. Note that this is a far cry from denying that the law of causality exists; rather, Hume was arguing that something as pivotal to our understanding of reality as causal relationships is a matter that human reason is unable to know. It is no wonder, then, that the eighteenth-century philosophical world was catapulted into an epistemological crisis.

We should recognize from this analysis, most importantly, that it is one thing to say, as Hume did, "I do not know (nor can I know) what caused this event," and it is quite another thing to say, as do those who think Hume demolished the law of causality, "*Nothing* has caused this event." Such absurdity cannot be held consistently for even one day. Yet it is almost always found in modern-day philosophical attempts to deny the existence of God. Those who deny causality usually replace it with some notion of "chance." Hume himself defined chance as a synonym for ignorance—that we appeal to chance as the "cause" of things we don't understand. What we can learn from Hume's critique is that sense perceptions are indeed limited, that given our limited knowledge of unseen causes, we will sometimes lack the sufficient ground to be sure that certain events share causal relationships. This critique therefore helps us with our humility, gently reminding us that we cannot prove causal relationships with some sort of supernatural infallibility. This by no means requires us, however, to jettison the law of causality, a formal principle that by definition is true—that if we are ever able to define an event as an effect, then we can be certain that that event has been caused by something other than itself.

Immanuel Kant and the Basic Reliability of Sense Perception

Given that Hume's critique of the law of causality sent his contemporaries into an epistemological crisis, this would be a good place to explore the third nonnegotiable principle of knowledge: the basic reliability of sense perception. Hume showed that our senses have limitations; that is, our powers of perception can never penetrate the invisible realm where perhaps various kinds of unseen forces (most significantly the providence of God) are in operation.

The apostle Paul quotes the stoic philosopher Epimenides, "In him we live and move and have our being" (Acts 17:28). Focusing on the second part of that statement, "In him we . . . move," we see that nothing can move in the universe apart from the providence of God. Even though we can cause many events to happen, ultimately, all matter moves by God's invisible power. Since there can be no motion apart from God, and since God is indeed invisible, no amount of empirical research will be able to *prove* that God is the first cause of every event. This is not to say, however, that empirical research cannot be compelling enough to *persuade*.

Christians should have no complaint with Hume's critique, insofar as we allow it to show the limits of human sense perception. Unfortunately, Hume attempted to reduce everything that involves using the senses (e.g., the natural sciences) to skepticism. That is, we cannot rely on our senses in our quest for truth. But if the senses are not reliable, it is not just Christian theism that falls; science collapses as well. This is why Hume's contemporary, Immanuel Kant (1724–1804), spent his entire career striving to revivify the validity of causal relationships and the basic reliability of sense perception. Kant rightly discerned that if these formative principles were demolished, all knowledge would be unattainable.

We are not arguing that our senses can give us an exhaustive or comprehensive understanding of reality; rather, we maintain only the basic reliability of our senses, that the link between our minds (what we think) and the external world (those objects outside of our minds) is reliable. Even though our senses are imperfect, they are nonetheless our only avenue to the physical world, the world outside our minds. The only doorway my mind has to the external world is my senses. The mind can think, imagine, or reflect. But it cannot perceive anything without the aid of the senses.

The basic reliability of our senses is nonnegotiable for modern scientists just as it is for biblical theologians. Peter assumes the same when he writes about the truth of the Messiah's coming:

> For we did not follow cleverly devised myths when we made known to you the power and coming of our Lord Jesus Christ, but we were *eyewitnesses* of his majesty. For when he received

> honor and glory from God the Father, and the voice was borne
> to him by the Majestic Glory, "This is my beloved Son, with
> whom I am well pleased," we ourselves *heard* this very voice
> borne from heaven, for we were with him on that holy moun-
> tain (2 Pet. 1:16-18, emphasis added).

Notice that the basic reliability of sense perception, the law of causality, and the law of noncontradiction are *all* assumed in this passage. If the senses were not reliable, why would Peter use his witnessing the events (both visually and audibly) as evidence for Christ? If causal relationships were not assumed, how could Christ have "received honor and glory" (an effect) from the voice "borne to him by the Majestic Glory" (a cause)? Finally, if the law of noncontradiction were not presupposed by Peter, then he would have seen no difference between "cleverly devised myths" and the events themselves. We should, therefore, take heed of these three principles and allow them to instruct and guide us in our apologetical task.

8

LOGICAL POSITIVISM AND ITS GHOSTS TODAY: ANALOGICAL USE OF LANGUAGE

The fourth and final formative principle of knowledge that we are discussing is the "analogical use of language." Even though this principle is probably the most esoteric to the layperson engaged in apologetics, it is nonetheless a fundamental issue that we all assume or else we embrace the absurd. Recall how the atheist typically denies the formative principles that we have discussed thus far. It should be no surprise, then, that this principle has also come under attack by those who reject classical theism. Their contention is with language itself, and whether it is a suitable means of communicating anything about the reality of God's existence.

Is It Possible to Know or Say Anything About God?

During the 1920s and 30s, philosophers in both European and American universities began focusing intently on human language. In the midst of this philosophical shift, an academic dispute known as the "God-talk controversy" erupted, resulting in a theological movement known as "Theo-thanatology." This was recapitulated as "the death of God" movement of the 1960s. Behind these controversies was the philosophical shift from metaphysics to language. When this shift reached Great Britain, it assumed the name "logical positivism," and one of its central tenets became known as "the principle of verification." This principle can be stated simply as: only those statements that can be empirically verified (i.e., by the scientific method) have any meaning. In other words, logical positivists argued that claims made with human language are true if and only if they can be proven through sense perception (seeing, hearing, touching, etc.). All other claims, they said, are emotional and unsupportable. For example, if someone declared that Alaska contained gold, the only way that statement could be proven empirically would be to go to Alaska, dig, find some gold, and show it to others who can see it, touch it, and so on.

Logical positivism enjoyed a wonderful welcome in the philosophical scene, making a tremendous impact on the academic community until one day a small voice pointed out what should have been obvious from the beginning: if the only statements that are true are statements that can be verified empirically, then the principle of verification itself would fail the test because its own premise, "only those statements that can be empirically verified have any meaning," cannot be empirically verified. The logical positivist school of thought retreated back into the halls of academia. Despite this defeat, however, the verification principle is still used by many nonbelievers as a tool of criticism against classical theism. Atheists usually reject any language that makes claims about God, on the grounds that such language cannot be proven scientifically.

This is critical to remember as we engage others in apologetics. We should also remember that it is exceedingly harder to *falsify* a statement (such as the statement that God exists) than it is to verify it. Let us go back to Alaska. If someone asserts that there is gold in Alaska and that he can verify it, all he would need to do is go to Alaska, find some gold, and show it to us. Now consider the opposite. What if someone claimed that there is *no* gold in Alaska? He would need to go to Alaska and excavate every square inch of that state and show us the results, namely, that no gold exists in Alaska. But how could the gold-digger be so sure that no tiny speck of gold was lost in the process of excavation? He would have to go back and do it again, and again, and again, *ad infinitum.* In other words, it is far more difficult to empirically falsify than it is to empirically verify. Many Christians take comfort in this fact. But they must be aware that even though God cannot be proven false, it does not follow from this that he is therefore proven true.

With logic, however, falsification is another (and somewhat simpler) matter entirely. If someone has an argument that in time is shown to violate the law of noncontradiction, then that argument is proven false. The difficulty increases, of course, when we start talking about God and his existence, mainly because no one today has seen or heard God, nor has any empirical evidence proven his existence. Our belief in God as Christians, though, is reinforced by rational arguments based upon inferences drawn from things that we can all see such as creation. We look at the cosmos, and deduce that there is a Creator above and beyond it, who made it and holds it together (e.g., Acts 17:28; Col. 1:17).

The skeptics in the middle of the twentieth century contended that since there is no *physical* proof for God, statements or claims about God are at best nonsensical and emotional. That is, when someone claims that he believes in God, logical positivists would argue that he is not saying anything meaningful about an *objective* God (a God who exists apart from creation), but is merely telling others about his own feelings. Since God cannot be verified empirically, they argue, believers have believed a lie of their own making. From this line of reasoning stems the ultimate in religious relativism, which often goes something like this: "God may exist for you but not for me." But as Christians we often fail to articulate precisely what kind of God we are arguing exists. When orthodox believers assert the existence of God, they are claiming that a supreme being exists outside of themselves, who is not a part of their thoughts or feelings and who is not created or changed by any actions wrought by human hands.

Relativistic nonbelievers fail to see that if this eternal God exists, then all of their unbelief combined lacks the power to annihilate him. When we are discussing the existence of God, we are asserting the objective existence of a God who exists apart from us as believing subjects. If he does not exist objectively, then all of our faith or feeling does not have the power to conjure him up. The logical positivists and those theologians who embraced Theo-thanatology, however, contended that all God-talk reduces to human emotions—statements that reveal only inner feelings, not an external reality. We will now briefly turn to the ideas that helped shape this radical skepticism.

Following the Enlightenment period of the eighteenth century, many theologians sought to integrate orthodox Christianity and the newest scientific discoveries, which most often resulted in emptying the faith of its many supernatural mysteries. Before long, liberal theologians rejected anything that transcended the natural order. Ancient biblical prophecies no longer foretold future events, they said; later editors had simply manipulated the manuscripts to look predictive. The virgin birth of the Messiah was rejected because it seemed naturally impossible. The atonement, far from being a cosmic event, was reduced to one man's delusional self-sacrifice. Indeed, every miracle became little more than fictional additions to the Scripture's nominal historicity. The only aspect of the Christian faith worth saving, so the liberals thought, was the ethical commands of Jesus. The entirety of the gospel message was found in the maxim "love your neighbor," which the liberals translated to mean progressive humanitarianism on earth without any thought of the supernatural.

This "natural" religion promoted by the liberals was coupled with the evolutionary philosophy of the late-nineteenth-century secularists. Historically, Christians have affirmed both the transcendence and immanence of God in relation to his creation. Simply put, God's *transcendence* refers to his being over and beyond the created order and superior to it in every way; his *immanence* refers to his ongoing actions within the created order.

The union between liberal theologians and evolutionary philosophy resulted in a heretical overemphasis on God's immanence, also known as *pantheism*. Within pantheistic theology, the balance between God's superiority and other-ness, and his ongoing providence, is completely lost. If God does exist, according to this view, then he exists as part and parcel of the universe itself—God is all things, and all things are God. But if God comprises the cosmos, the word *God* cannot refer to anything in *particular* because it would refer to everything in *general*. So, along with this extreme immanence came a crisis of language that challenged anyone who attempted to speak meaningfully about God.

And then the pendulum swung. At the beginning of the twentieth century, European theologians reacted against the accommodating liberalism and attempted to revitalize the transcendence of God. Unfortunately, they over-corrected the problem, arguing that God is "wholly other." In other words, God is so separated from the universe that not only is he disassociated from the created order, existing above it, but he exists totally above and beyond nature to such an extent that his creation can never hope to gain any knowledge about him whatsoever. God is, as the German philosopher Rudolf Otto said, *ganze andere*—completely different. In their (albeit well-intentioned) attempt to combat the radical immanence of the previous generation, these theologians contributed to an equally damaging crisis regarding language and its use as a valid form of communication about God.

Our Analogical Knowledge of God

Karl Barth (1886–1968), in his *Church Dogmatics*, popularized this overemphasis on God's transcendence. He also vehemently assaulted the use of natural theology in apologetics and its attempts to learn about the living God from deductions drawn from nature, mainly because he opposed invoking the liberal theologian's idea of reason while doing theology. Barth's antipathy toward reason and natural theology, however, was aimed not only at the liberals of his own day but at a deeply rooted prin-

ciple within historic Christianity—the *analogia entis*—articulated
most clearly by Thomas Aquinas (1225–1274) during his years at
the University of Paris. The *analogia entis,* or "analogy of being,"
is simply the idea that God and man share a relationship (as we
are his image-bearers), which establishes the use of "analogy"
as a way for finite man to speak about the infinite God. This
is exactly what Barth and the other neo-orthodox theologians
attacked: since God completely transcends the created order, he is
therefore totally different from his creation, making any analogy
of being between the Creator and the created impossible. While
Barth and the other neo-orthodox theologians were guarding
against the liberals' rabid redefinition of God, their unintended
consequence was the construction of a chasm so wide that not
even the Creator could cross over into the realm of humanity.
This rendered any discussion about God entirely irrelevant. As
soon as we describe God as "wholly other" we open the door to
the skeptic who rightly derides us for talking about God when we
have no right to, because the skeptic understands that if there is
no similarity between the Creator and creature, then there is no
possible avenue of communication about him.

By way of illustration, consider the meaning of the word
chair. What comes to mind? Granted, we all might picture in our
minds a different chair, but we all share a common understanding regarding chairs in general. Many of us have seen hundreds
of thousands of chairs in our lifetime, depending on our respective ages. Every time we see objects that resemble chairs, we then
make the connection between the object and its function, namely,
to hold us as we sit. Along with our recognizing the object and its
function, we associate the word *chair* with the object itself. From
our varied and repeated experiences with chairs comes our understanding of the word *chair*. We know what a chair is, because we
have experienced over and over again the act of sitting in one.
Styles may change, as well as our individual experiences, but our
experiences with chairs are nonetheless so overwhelmingly *similar*
that the differences in our understandings of the word *chair* are

irrelevant. In other words, the reader knows what is meant when he or she reads the word *chair*. In order to carry on a meaningful conversation we must, at the very least, basically understand the words being used.

The same principle applies in theology, and especially in the task of apologetics. If there is no common ground between man and God, then anything he has said to his creation is completely unintelligible. But such is not the case. When, for example, orthodox Christians assert (from the Bible) that God is omnipotent, we can know something about omnipotence even though we have never encountered a fully omnipotent being on this earth. The word itself means "all-powerful," and "power" is a word we all understand because we all at one time or another have exerted power over something else. Even though our power is limited, we can still imagine what unlimited power might be like, mainly because we see degrees of power in the world that surrounds us (i.e., we see that some things are more powerful than other things). Therefore, when God reveals himself in the Bible as omnipotent, we at least have some concept of power that enables us to apprehend what the word means. This point of contact, however, is possible only if there is some sense in which God is like us and we are like him—that is, only if there is an analogy of being between us and God.

The issue of the meaningfulness and adequacy of God-talk is not new. Thomas Aquinas dealt with the same question in the thirteenth century. As a defender of the Christian faith from Muslim relativists, Aquinas distinguished among three kinds or uses of language: *univocal, equivocal,* and the middle way—*analogical.* Taking the word *good* as an example should help us better understand Aquinas's use of these terms. In the statements "Good work on the painting," and "Good work on the cutting," the word *good* is used *univocally,* that is, in an identical sense. A word is used *equivocally* if it is used in two entirely different senses. For example, in the statements "That sermon was good," and "Good grief, Charlie Brown!" the two words share no similarity at all.

Words or things have an *analogical* relationship when they
are partly alike and partly different—neither univocal nor equivocal. They share a relationship of similarity but not identity
between the meaning of a term when attributed to one subject
("This chili is good") and the meaning of that term when attributed to another subject ("God is good"). Imagine that a dog and
its owner are playing in the park. The owner says, "Bingo, you're
a good dog." Now imagine that two of the dog owner's friends
happen to be in the park at the same time and see him from a
distance. "He's a good guy," one of the friends remarks to the
other. Is the dog "good" in the exact same sense that its owner
is? That is, does the dog have the highly developed sense of conscience and ethical imperative that the owner might have? No.
The dog comes when called, is house-broken, and doesn't bite
the mailman on the leg. But when we say the dog's owner is a
"good guy," we mean something more than that he comes when
he is called, is housebroken, and doesn't bite the mailman on the
leg. The owner's goodness is directly proportionate to his being
human; the dog's "goodness" is proportionate to its being an ani-
mal. The two "goods" are not identical but they are analogical.

The same principle applies in our talking about the goodness
of God. Just as our goodness is in some sense akin to God's goodness, one dissimilarity remains: his goodness far exceeds ours.
When orthodox Christians affirm God's goodness, they are not
using the word *good* in a univocal sense; rather, they are using
it analogically. And analogical language is meaningful because
God has created humans in his image (Gen. 1:27), thereby giving
us, in the act of Creation, an analogy of being—the very grounds
upon which God's communication to us becomes significant and
intelligible. Humans were given a distinctive nature and place in
the created order (Gen. 5:3; 1 Cor. 15:39), being in the "image
and glory of God" (1 Cor. 11:7), which included dominion over
everything on earth (Gen. 1:26, 28). Being in the image of God
also means resembling him to some degree. We, like God, can rest
(Gen. 2:2), talk (Ex. 6:10-11) and reason (Isa. 1:18), for example.

Our dominion over creation as God's stewards also mirrors his own sovereign governing (Ps. 95:3-6). Without this bond, we could have no understanding of the created world and its testimony to the greatness of the Creator's hand. What is more, we could have no understanding of God's special revelation through the Word—both written and made flesh in Jesus Christ his Son.

Virtually every attack against theism involves a rejection of one or more of the four basic necessary principles for human knowledge: 1) the law of noncontradiction, 2) the law of causality, 3) the basic reliability of sense perception, 4) the adequacy of human language to communicate. All four of these principles are assumed throughout the Bible. They are also assumed in the scientific method. They are all necessary instruments for knowledge—indeed for all science.

All denials of these basic principles are *forced* and *temporary*. People deny them only when they have a vested interest in their denial. But these denials do not last long. They cannot last long, for these principles are necessary for surviving as living creatures.

SECTION III
Natural Reason
and Faith

NATURAL THEOLOGY AND SCIENCE

The whole notion of natural theology endured an aggressive assault during this past century. Some critics, such as Karl Barth, argued that natural theology was a dangerous endeavor to engage in, because if we attempt to learn about the living God from deductions drawn from nature, the probability that we will end up with a god made after our own image is greatly increased. It is important to keep in mind that Barth was reacting against the nineteenth-century liberals who were doing just that. Barth argued that God cannot be manipulated by our own finite inferences from the created world. Barth's concern was valid. But his theology had unfortunate consequences affecting our very ability to say anything positive about the triune God. We must not take it as far as Barth. Still other critics contended that while natural theology can be done, it can never be done rightly. That is to say, natural theology is entirely irrelevant, for man can gain nothing by seeking knowledge of God from nature. Man is fallen and unable to comprehend such things. In other words, God's revelation in creation is inaccessible to sinners. This view takes human depravity too far.

When the term *natural theology* is used, the name immediately associated with it is Thomas Aquinas, wrongly understood to be the originator of this concept. I contend, however, that Aquinas stood largely on the shoulders of Augustine of Hippo, who in turn labored to understand and apply the teachings of the apostle Paul himself.

Natural Theology Comes from General Revelation

"Natural theology" is discourse about God *informed by* our knowledge of nature. It is a knowledge of God gained through an understanding of the external world, in addition to and distinct from the knowledge of God available to us in the Holy Scriptures. Natural theology traditionally has been based on what theologians call *general revelation*. General revelation is God's self-disclosure in his created universe. This revelation is an objective act of God that does not rely on our perception of it in order to be true. *Natural theology* is the human response to general revelation. Natural theology is a human act, a way for us to understand God's revelation of himself in creation. General *revelation* is what God does; natural *theology* is what we do with that revelation.

General revelation must be further distinguished from *special* revelation in two ways: 1) general revelation has been given to all people, that is, to a general audience—comprising all of humanity; 2) the content that this revelation imparts about God is general, not specific. For example, we can see evidences that a supreme being has created the universe, but we do not see that the being is triune, nor do we see a plan of redemption anywhere in the created order. To learn these things we need more than general revelation. We need the information found in *special* revelation. Not everyone has had the benefit of hearing the special revelation found in God's Word. Many isolated tribes, not to mention the average citizen in the post-Christian West, have never heard the stories of the Bible and the redemption it reveals. General revelation covers the whole earth, while special revelation does not.

General revelation can be distinguished into two different kinds: *mediate* and *immediate*. *Mediate* general revelation refers to God's revelation of himself through some type of medium.

The medium is nature itself. Consider the following excerpt from Psalm 19:

> The heavens declare the glory of God,
>   and the sky above proclaims his handiwork.
> Day to day pours out speech,
>   and night to night reveals knowledge (vv. 1-2).

The psalmist sings the glories of God as revealed in the skies above. The heavens proclaim God's handiwork; day after day, night after night, in the beautiful arrangement of time, the glory of the Creator God resounds in the heavens. The stars, the moon, indeed, all of the universe displays the glory of its Maker. As painters leave something of themselves on their canvases (their medium of choice), so God, when creating the universe, left an indelible mark of glory on all that is.

Immediate general revelation, on the other hand, refers to that revelation of God that comes to us *directly,* without any intermediary such as the external, created world. It is not immediate in the sense that it happens quickly or suddenly; rather it is immediate in that this general revelation is written on the minds and hearts of every human being. God's law is written on our hearts (Rom. 2:15), which is the true conscience embraced by the godly and suppressed by the wicked. Each person coming into this world carries an innate sense of God, put there by God himself. By virtue of being created in his image, we carry an intuitive sense that God exists, a deduction not drawn from nature but from our own souls. Calvin called this the *divinitatis sensum,* or the "awareness of divinity" residing in all people.[1] Despite the Fall, the image of God, though devastated, resides unmovable in human hearts. Paul leaves no room for excuses: all people can understand at the very least a most basic concept of their Creator, namely, that he exists and therefore demands their thanksgiving.

Paul's letter to the Romans gives the church its clearest teaching on general revelation: "For the wrath of God is revealed from heaven against all ungodliness and unrighteousness of men . . ." (1:18a). This passage, as well as the passages that follow, are somewhat striking, not just because of their profundity but because of their placement in the letter. Paul has just written about how faith leads the believer into the righteous life, for the gospel is "the power of God for salvation" (vv. 16-17). The reader might expect the apostle to continue this grand theme. After all, he is writing to Christians. But he jarringly begins writing about another revelation—not a revelation of the glorious good news of the Messiah for those who believe, but a revelation of God's *wrath*. There is one obvious reason that Paul does this: to show his readers why the gospel is necessary in the first place. The necessity of Christ's coming for our salvation pre-supposes the universal guilt of all humanity, and so Paul goes back a few steps in order to show why everyone faces God's wrath. In chapter 3 of Romans, he further hammers down the point that "all have sinned and fall short of the glory of God" (v. 23). Therefore, every person to have ever lived needs the gospel—not because they have simply rejected Jesus, of whom many have never heard—but because of what all people have done with the knowledge of God they already possess.

Continuing with our text, "For the wrath of God is revealed from heaven against all ungodliness and unrighteousness of men, who by their unrighteousness suppress the truth" (Rom. 1:18). We need a savior because we have suppressed the truth. This is the single sin in view here: the ungodly, unrighteous sin of suppression of truth. It is the definitive sin of all people in all ages: the suppression, not of "truth" in general but of *the* truth in particular, namely, "what can be known about God is plain to them, because God has shown it to them" (v. 19). The truth all sinners suppress, which exacts the wrath of God, is knowledge about the Creator. Is there any wiggle-room left for the one who suppresses this truth? "For [God's] invisible attributes, namely, his eternal power and divine nature, have been clearly perceived, ever since the creation of the world, in the things that have been made. So they are without excuse" (v. 20). Ever since the creation of this world, Paul writes, the Creator has plainly revealed himself in his Creation. It is not a hidden revelation; rather, it is clear and perceptible, and not just to the educated but even to the child. Everyone to have ever lived can see it, and therefore we are all without excuse.

Maybe Paul intended to silence the grumbling of those who will stand before God in judgment, who will cry that this is all unfair: "If only we had known you were actually there, God, then we would have worshiped and adored you." But God, through his apostle, expresses that he will not entertain such excuses, for all people have known that he is there. When they have not followed him, it was not because they failed to see his general revelation in creation but because they hated him and refused to think of him at all. This indictment covers the whole world, from its inception to its end.

Some people conceive of this singular sin as follows: God does indeed reveal himself clearly in creation, but as a result of our corrupted nature, this revelation is not grasped. The objective manifestation of the Creator's hand never pierces the mind of the creature. God's revelation cannot be seen by natural man because of sin. This, however, is not what Paul taught when he wrote the letter. It is not that people refuse to allow the clear revelation of God in nature into their heads; quite the contrary, the revelation does indeed get through. The basis of the indictment is that while the people *know* God, they still do "not honor him as God or give thanks to him" (Rom. 1:21a). The manifestation of the Creator's existence in his creation is clearly perceived by the minds of all people. The problem is that this knowledge is continually distorted and suppressed, until finally the truth is exchanged for a lie (vv. 21-32). Not only does God act objectively through his creation, which produces a general revelation of himself, this revelation goes on to produce a natural *theology* that serves as the basis for the universal guilt of all mankind.

One of the most common objections to such theology comes in the question, "What happens to the poor, innocent people in the wilderness who have never heard the gospel?" The appropriate response to this type of question ought to be, "Nothing. Nothing whatsoever happens to poor innocent people, for they do not even need to hear the gospel. The innocent people go straight to heaven when they die. There is no worry for them. In fact, mission work for innocent people ought to be abolished immediately." *Innocent* people do not need the gospel ("I have not come to call the righteous but sinners to repentance" Luke 5:32). The real question we ought to ask first when grappling with natural theology is, "How many 'innocent' people *are* there out in the wilderness?" If we rightly understand the apostle to the Gentiles (who, by the way, preached to people who were completely unaware of the Good News), then we would see that there are no "innocent" people, nor have there ever been any "innocent" people in the entire history of the world, for all people have received a clear revelation of the Creator. Every one of them has suppressed this knowledge, refusing to give him thanks and choosing to worship anything but the living God. It is to this world, a world already under the curse of God's wrath, that the Father sent his Son to be a propitiation for sins. Natural theology, then, in its most basic sense, is that knowledge of God that every human has had—since the beginning of creation—as a direct consequence of general revelation, or that knowledge gained about God through nature. This natural theology is the basis for universal guilt; no one can plead ignorance as an excuse for not obeying God.

Understanding Aquinas: Nature and Grace

We must be cautious on this point, and not compound the misunderstandings that surround Aquinas and his exposition of natural theology. Aquinas, as we mentioned earlier, stood on Augustine's shoulders. But he also went to Romans 1—just like Augustine before him. Critics of Aquinas have wrongly accused him of teaching something to the effect that man, through unaided reason (the intellect with which he was born—without any assistance from divine revelation), has the mental capacity to reason himself or herself into the heavens, arriving at a knowledge of God. This is not what Aquinas, Augustine, or Paul taught. Natural theology, all three of them asserted, comes by way of God's general revelation in nature. Its origin is divine. Man, being born into this world, does not need to rely on "unaided reason," for since the creation of the world, God's "invisible attributes, namely, his eternal power and divine nature, have been clearly perceived" (Rom. 1:20a).

Nonetheless, Aquinas turned out to be the Protestant punching bag of the twentieth century. In like manner, natural theology is seen by many Protestants to be inherently Roman Catholic and therefore incompatible with any theology not explicitly Catholic. To make matters worse, Aquinas, in more recent years, has been accused of contributing to a specific theological and philosophical crisis: the separation of grace from nature. The idea that Aquinas supposedly promulgated is that grace exists in a transcendent realm above nature; the two, nature and grace, are hopelessly separated by a barrier. This, some argue, is why reason is often seen as being opposed to faith—the natural versus the supernatural. But our defense of Aquinas rests on the exact opposite of this supposed separation. In fact, the intended result of Aquinas's entire philosophical enquiry was to show the ultimate *union* between nature and grace. The last thing he wanted to do was separate the two; indeed, such an accusation betrays a serious misunderstanding of the historical context within which Aquinas taught, and of his actual teaching.

During the twelfth century, an Arabian thinker by the name of Averroës (1126–1198) was busy adapting Aristotle's philosophy to the Islamic religion. About this same time, Aristotle's works were translated from Greek into Latin, enabling many Westerners to join in on the study of Aristotelian philosophy. Averroës and his followers found themselves in conflict with a few tenets of Islam as a result of their accommodation to Aristotle. For example, Averroës came to believe (as did Aristotle) that the world was eternal rather than having a distinct beginning in time. As the his-

tory of Islam shows, Islamic leaders were not especially friendly
to those who snubbed the official doctrine. To get around this
potentially life-threatening circumstance, Averroës promulgated
a "double theory of truth," which suggested that a premise could
be true in philosophy and false in theology at the same time (or
vice versa). This apparently cleared him from suspicion.

We should stop here for a moment and consider the parallels
of this concept with today's forms of relativism. Simply stated,
the double theory of truth taught the opposite of the law of noncontradiction. While the double theory argued that something
could be true in religion and false in philosophy, the law of noncontradiction, as we have already seen, teaches that *A* cannot be
A and non-*A* at the same time and in the same sense. To adapt it
to our purposes here, God could not *be* the creator of the world
and *not be* the creator of the world at the same time and in the
same sense. Either he was or he was not. Today, we might find
Christians who affirm that God both did and did not have a hand
in Creation. That is, in the context of their work or profession,
they believe that the universe is a result of a gratuitous collision of atoms; and yet in their relationship to the church, they
believe that God created the universe by divine fiat. On Sunday
they believe God created the heavens and the earth, and the rest
of the week they believe that the universe has evolved slowly,
"starting" an incalculable number of years in the past. Averroës
and the other Islamic philosophers argued in this same fashion—
that, depending on which perspective we are coming from, both
theories are equally true. If we are looking at the origin of the
universe scientifically, then eternal evolution is true; if we are
looking at the origin of the universe theologically, then creation
by God is true.

In the thirteenth century, Averroism spread to the West and
began infecting many of the great universities as soon as they were
founded. Despite the church's attempt to discipline such teachings,
the movement grew strong at the University of Paris under Siger
of Brabant (1235–1282). The difference at this point was that

these Averroists worked under the auspices of the Roman church. Many of them, including Siger, were known to have rejected the doctrine of Creation as well as the doctrine of the immortality of the soul. To escape banishment, they claimed the double theory of truth. It was upon this scene that the Doctor of the Church, Thomas Aquinas, entered. In order to refute these enemies of the church, Aquinas constructed his apologetic of natural theology. As he did, he went on to make a distinction (not a separation) between nature and grace, science and theology, faith and reason. We must maintain, however, that separation and distinction are two different things. Aquinas's critics argue that he *separated* the two, that he believed it was impossible for the realm of science and the realm of theology to intersect. In other words, he is said to have believed that the knowledge we gain through the sciences is *not* dependent upon any graceful revelation whatsoever. But most also agree that despite his "separating" nature from grace, there was one major exception—the existence of God. The simple fact that a Creator exists, said Aquinas, can be known equally in both spheres. We will return to this shortly. But first, we will discuss how Aquinas made the distinction (not separation) between nature and grace.

To begin with, there are certain things that we can learn from nature that we do not learn from grace (and vice versa). For example, the Bible does not teach us astronomy, as the Holy Spirit had no intention to inform us about how the universe "runs" but rather how the universe has fallen under the curse of sin and is in desperate need of redemption. "The Bible tells us how to go to heaven," Galileo wrote, "not how the heavens go."[2] This, of course, came from a man censured and placed on house arrest by the Roman Inquisition for merely describing what he saw through a telescope. To further examine this point, we can learn through science that the moon reflects light, but to our eyes it looks like a generator of light, and the Bible in fact describes it as such (Gen. 1:14-19). Is the Word of God therefore wrong? No, because its author was not intending to teach us about the moon's reflecting of the sun's light but rather about how God divided the days from the nights, a temporal device used by the Creator to bring his people to rest on the Sabbath (Gen. 2:1-3). Our study of science enhances our knowledge of the world around us in ways the Bible does not address. Likewise, the Bible teaches us God's way of salvation, a path that no scientific study could ever uncover. The following excerpt from Aquinas's *Summa Theologica* should all but silence the critics who accuse him of deeply dividing nature and grace:

> It seems that a man cannot know any truth without grace. . . . Now however pure it be, bodily sense cannot see any visible thing without the light of the sun. Hence however perfect be the human mind, it cannot by reasoning know any truth without the light of God, which belongs to the aid of grace. . . . The natural light bestowed on the mind is God's light, by which we are enlightened to know such things as belong to natural knowledge.[3]

How much more clearly does Aquinas have to state the matter? The knowledge that we gain in the sphere of science is entirely dependent on the bestowal of God's light on the mind. Just as we can see nothing in a dark room, without the light of God we can see no truth. In Aquinas's thought, then, it should be increasingly clear that nature and grace are complementary, not opposed. There is no such thing, according to Aquinas, as autonomous reason, that is, reason unaided by divine revelation. For Aquinas, our very use of intellect is a result of God's grace. Those who accuse him otherwise must fail to see the important difference between a "distinction" and a "separation."

One final distinction that Aquinas made must be discussed, for it is the one around which so much controversy exists. In addition to the two distinct types of knowledge that can be gained from science or the Bible, there are a few articles of information that can be learned from *both* science and the Bible. Chief among these "mixed articles," says Aquinas, is the existence of God.

The existence of this world's Creator can be surmised through a study of nature as well as from the Bible. In other words, one does not have to read the Bible in order to know that God exists. Aquinas was, after all, a proponent of natural theology, and so he affirmed that the Bible itself teaches that its pages are not the only way that God's existence can be known; rather the Bible teaches that God's existence can also be known "in the things that have been made" by him (Rom. 1:20). Some apologists might object, however, by citing Genesis 1:1a, which reads, "In the beginning God . . ." Their point would be that the Bible at its very outset already assumes that God exists; should not we likewise, at the outset of our apologetic task, just assume that God exists? But for the Bible to argue for the existence of its author would be completely unnecessary. Why? Because of natural theology. Ages before the first words of Scripture were ever written down, God had clearly revealed himself in nature. The Creator's existence had been conclusively proven through his creation. By the time anyone is old enough to read from the sacred Scriptures, he or she already has both God's eternal power and his divine nature clearly revealed in the things he has made. For this reason, Aquinas (and Augustine before him) argued that the existence of God can be demonstrated both by nature and by grace. Therefore, the two corresponding spheres of enquiry, science and theology, so far from being separated and opposed to one another, are actually in perfect agreement—because all truth is God's truth. Science and theology both presuppose God's divine revelation; and they both meet, as it were, at the top.

Science and Theology: Why the Conflict?

But how do we explain the fact that the scientific and religious communities have frequently found themselves in conflict with each other, especially in the modern era? Indeed, as far as the general population is concerned, science and religion are seen as being completely at odds. In an ideal world, of course, there would be no such conflict between reason and faith, nature and

grace. And this was Aquinas's point: even though we do not
live in an ideal world, nature and grace are nonetheless entirely
complementary. If a theory is false in science, then it must be
false in theology as well (and vice versa). Obviously, the problem
is that *sinners* are doing both the science and the theology. On
one side, scientists are prone to mistakes, to reading the data
wrong, according to bias; and on the other side, the same applies
to the theologian. During the sixteenth century, virtually everyone thought that the earth was the center of the solar system.
Copernicus was the "devil's agent," and it was not just the pope
and his bishops who thought this; Luther and Calvin thought the
same—that Copernicus had somehow undermined the integrity
of Scripture. But Copernicus not only proved his position, he
proved that the Roman church's official teaching on the subject
was wrong. What he did not do, and this is very important to
remember, is correct the teachings of Scripture; rather, he cor-
rected the church's *misunderstanding* of Scripture. The church
leaders had, in effect, treated the Bible as an astronomy manual,
and as a result had produced glaringly unsound doctrine. This
does not mean, however, that every time a conflict arises between
science and theology, the scientists are right. On the contrary, the
scientist is just as susceptible to poor judgments as the theologian. When a scientist, for example, wants to argue that the entire
universe is evolving slowly as a result of atoms randomly slam-
ming into one another, the church has an obligation to correct
the scientist. In today's post-Christian culture, however, religion
is relegated to the private sphere. If church leaders rise up and
declare falsehood when they see it, the world throws a tantrum:
"How dare you impose your beliefs upon me. You can believe
religion if you want, but do it in your own house!" So barks
the world at the church today. Religion, says the unbeliever, is
nothing more than subjective opinions, and truth can be found
only through the scientific method. But Aquinas serves as a model
for us today in this regard. He stood up to his opponents at the
University of Paris and chided them for being the irrational ones.

The epitome of rationality, argued Aquinas, is recognizing that science drives us conclusively and compellingly toward the existence of God. The Scriptures and science proclaim the same truth. They support each other because God's revelation of himself in nature is just as true as his revelation of himself in Scripture. The Scriptures and science are united—not without their distinctions, of course—but united. To separate them is to do exactly what the world does. Aquinas did no such thing, and is not deserving of the accusation. Showing the complementary nature of science and religion is precisely what Aquinas attempted. Like Augustine before him, Aquinas understood that wherever truth is found, the truth of God is being discovered. It should be no surprise to us if science and theology are abused—after all, we are corrupt in our thinking. What should surprise us is the timidity with which the Christian community has received its banishment to the private sector. Our duty is to stand up, as Aquinas did, and expose the abuses that follow once nature has been separated from grace. Instead, we have bought the modern lie, that the church has nothing valid to say to the world.

10

AQUINAS AND KANT

Looking as we have at Thomas Aquinas, the "Angelicus Doctor" (a title conferred upon him in the 1560s), we see that God raises individuals, fallen though they may be, to fight for the gospel so that false teaching within the church may be confronted. Never do these moments of balance last very long, however. New thinkers come along—some good, some bad—all of whom are mostly unaware of the ethical consequences their philosophies will have. Such was the case for Immanuel Kant. It was Kant, not Aquinas, who separated grace from nature. We will explore how he did just that.

From the time of Aquinas until the time of Kant (about five hundred years), the traditional arguments for the existence of God enjoyed a supremacy that was rarely challenged. In fact, they seemed so persuasive to the minds of most scholars that the whole notion of God's existence was seldom disputed. The first and most famous of these arguments is called, among other things, the *ontological* argument for the existence of God. It assumes various shades and nuances—about as many as there are intellectuals who use it in their own arguments. We will discuss this in more detail later, but for now we need to see that the Greek prefix *onto-* simply means "being," so that the ontological argument focuses on what it means *to be* "God." Its most famous version comes to us from Saint Anselm, archbishop of Canterbury from 1093 to 1109, who, while not calling it the "ontological argument," articulated and refined the argument in his *Proslogium,* as well as in his reply to Gaunilo, his staunchest critic at the time.[1] The next traditional argument—called the *cosmological* argument—was summarized most notably by Aquinas. It essentially argued from the law of causality: the world, or cosmos, being an unnecessary effect (that is, it does not *have* to exist), must have had a cause, since nothing can cause itself. The world that we perceive with our senses must therefore have a necessary first cause, otherwise known as the Creator God (see our earlier discussion on Hume, etc.). Another argument, called the *teleological* argument, is simply an argument from design (*telos*, from the Greek, means "in the end," "purpose," or "goal"). Today, for example, there is the debate between creationists and evolutionists regarding the origin of the universe. Basically, creationists argue against the evolutionary theory by contending that the cosmos displays an intelligent design. This is in many ways the old teleological argument: we observe many occasions of design in the world, which leads us to understand that an intelligent designer exists. In addition to these arguments, there was also a *moral* argument for the existence God, which we will look at in chapter 17.

In the Middle Ages especially, Christianity gained dominance in the Western hemisphere through the many Christian philosophers who defended the existence of God with the various formidable proofs for his existence. Theology was seen as the "queen of the sciences" in the medieval universities, and philosophy was her handmaiden, that is, her servant in the quest for sound theology. This presupposed a unity between theological affirmations and philosophical thinking and evidence, not to mention the elevated status of theological studies. Aquinas's synthesis of Aristotle's logic (from natural reason) and faith (supernatural grace) enjoyed a dominant position in theoretical thought for hundreds of years until Kant's colossal work, the *Critique of Pure Reason*, appeared in 1781.

Kant's Critique of Pure Reason

In the history of Western philosophy, Kant's *Critique* stands as a watershed moment. Revolutionary in scope, the book appeared just a few years after another monumental revolution, the American revolt against the crown of England. But Kant's intellectual revolution reached farther than any political upheaval ever could. In just the philosophical realm, Kant's thought influenced many subsequent philosophers, and many today define themselves by delineating the places where they agree or disagree with him.

Early in his philosophical training, Kant had been influenced by the popular rationalism of his day, a movement that subjected all knowledge (of both the world and God) to the test of human reason. *Rationalists* assert that the mind has authority over the five senses in determining truth. They also usually affirm that there are objective first principles of knowledge without which no knowledge is possible. (Recall our discussion of such principles in chapters 3-8.) During Kant's day, *empiricism* was also a dominant philosophy. Empiricism asserted that all ideas are based in *sense* experience (as opposed to the mind—contra rationalism). In other words, empiricists believed that the mind is blank upon birth into this world, and that it fills with knowledge through our experiences.

Kant sought to synthesize these two philosophies. He became disillusioned with the whole rationalistic enterprise, and after grappling with David Hume's critique of causality, he wrote that he had been "awakened" from his "dogmatic slumbers."[2] This awakening drove him to reevaluate what Hume's analysis had overthrown: the ability of sense experiences to lead us to ultimate truths (e.g., induction, from the law of causality, that God is the first cause). He wanted, at the very least, to restore the physical sciences to some degree of certainty. But along the way, in his attempted rescue of science from skepticism, Kant ended up attacking the traditional arguments for God's existence because he thought that Christianity had degenerated into a destructive dependence upon human reason, while undermining the aspect of believing in faith. His critique, then, was not atheistic; rather, it was an attempt to knock down the haughtiness of human reason so that room could be made for faith.

In *Critique of Pure Reason,* his most famous work, Kant set out to discover what knowledge comes to us as a result of our experiences (empiricism), such as our experience of the heat of fire, and what knowledge is independent of our experiences (rationalism), such as, for example, our concept of time. Basically, Kant ends up arguing that all of our knowledge comes as a result of both, except with the following twist: the knowledge we have that is independent of our experiences is purely mental and subjective, as opposed to an objective gift of God given to all humans. And since all of our knowledge comes from a combination of experience and reason working together, we can never come to know anything without it first being subjected to or filtered through our own understanding. Remember our analogy of the pool hall? Hume argued that we could never be sure that the pool player had sunk the eight ball, because our senses are essentially unable to justify such a determination. Kant would argue that our knowledge of the cause behind the sinking of the eight ball—the pool player—is a direct result of our mind disposing us to think in terms of the law of causality. In other words, we think the pool player is the cause simply because our minds already think in terms of cause and effect. Or to put it yet another way, the pool player appears to be the cause *to us*—and to us alone. That is, we cannot figure out the whole pool hall scene *as it really is,* only as it is *to us.* Norman Geisler puts it this way: "If Kant was right, we know how we know, but we no longer really know."[3] He is saying that if Kant was correct about how we come to know things, then that is all we will ever know, for we can never know anything else as it really is but only as it appears to us. Without the pool hall scene being filtered through our own understanding, we could make no sense of the player, the cue, the table, the ball, and so on. It appears to us a certain way, but the reality of it remains elusive. This is where we see Kant's radical separation between nature and grace take shape. Since our knowledge can never include things outside of the world as it appears to us, the world as it really is can never be known. The "world as it is" Kant calls the *noumenal* world; the "world as it appears," he calls the *phenomenal* world. The first one is above and beyond our ability to know; the second one is the world in which we live.

Within the noumenal realm, Kant placed three concepts: the ideas of God, the self, and the "thing-in-itself" (or a "thing as it really is," independent of our experiences). This third concept is, of course, the most difficult to understand. Kant basically meant that the metaphysical realm is beyond our abilities to ever perceive. For example, when we see a tree, we see its outward appearance—e.g., the bark, leaves, branches—not its "treeness." We cannot perceive such things as that. Again, when we come into contact with other people, we cannot observe their souls, we can only perceive them as they appear to us, that is, in their outward appearances. Many philosophers have postulated that such metaphysical realities were beyond the realm of physics (they were *meta*, or "beyond," the physical realm), and that they cannot be known by seeing, hearing, touching, tasting, or smelling. But most of these philosophers also argued that things in the metaphysical realm can nonetheless be known, whether by intuition alone or by a combination of intuition and experience. Kant argued, however, that those things were a part of the noumenal world. Things like God, for example, we cannot observe with the five senses; nor can we observe (with the five senses) our own minds, or the essences of material objects (like trees). Such things are strictly unknowable. In this way, Kant chopped off our ability to know anything beyond the observable world.

Kant nowhere claims to be an atheist, or that there are no such things as the self or the "thing-in-itself." For Kant, the question is epistemological. In response to Hume's challenge (that the physical sciences cannot conclusively lead to any ultimate truths), Kant was forced to ask, "What can I really know? If rational-empirical observation cannot inform me of metaphysical realities, what does? Or, can we know anything about metaphysical realities at all (like God, the self, etc.)?" His answer, unfortunately, was no. All of our knowledge is restricted to the physical realm, the realm of phenomena. The *phenomenal* world we are speaking of does not mean the "terrific" world; rather, it has to do with the world of appearances, or the world that can be perceived with the five senses. In most dictionaries, "phenomenon" means simply an object or aspect known through any of the five senses, as opposed to being known by thought or by intuition. Kant was saying that through empirical (scientific) observation we cannot get from the phenomenal world to the noumenal world. There is an unbridgeable chasm between the world that we see and the world as it really is. It follows, then, that we can have no knowledge whatsoever of the noumenal world. As a result of this serious separation between the phenomenal world and the noumenal world, Kant's challenge against the traditional arguments for the existence of God essentially condenses into an attack upon the use of natural theology. We have argued that all humans are endowed with a natural intellect capable of recognizing the existence of the Creator simply by virtue of being created in his image (cf. Rom. 1:18-21). But Kant argued that knowledge of God's existence cannot be attained through the use of reason, because (and here he bought into Hume's critique) we cannot be sure that principles such as the law of causality can be applied to the noumenal world, even though that same law can be used here in the phenomenal world. Reasoning toward the existence of God using the law of cause-and-effect, for Kant, was impossible. For this reason, Kant was skeptical about our ability to know anything about God (by way of the traditional arguments, at least).

So, why did Kant continue believing in God? For practical purposes, of course. Kant argued in his second most famous work, *Critique of Practical Reason,* that we must live as if there is a God, for if he did not exist, then we could make no judgments about right and wrong, good or evil. In order for civilization to be possible, there must be a God. If there is no way to differentiate between moral and immoral acts, then society will not endure; it will ultimately degenerate into anarchy. As one of Dostoevsky's characters contended, if there is no God, "then there's no virtue, and everything is lawful."[4] We will return to Kant's moral argument for God in chapter 17.

The Answer to Kant: Fideism, or Romans 1?

In the centuries that followed Kant's critiques of the traditional arguments for God's existence, many theologians and philosophers faced a radical skepticism, and, being unable to withstand it, were driven to detest natural theology and embrace various shades of *fideism*. Fideism, as we have seen, is the belief that the idea of God's existence is to be assumed on faith; given that God's existence cannot be known rationally, and given that his existence cannot be proven rationally, we must therefore accept his existence through a blind leap of faith. God, to the fideist, is to be assumed as a first principle upon which everything else is built. The fideist's assumption of God's existence is like the four formative principles we discussed in previous chapters in that it is a starting point for epistemological study. It is *unlike* our formative principles, however, in that we have *not* assumed our four principles in a blind leap of faith; rather, our whole point in discussing them was to show that they can be rationally accepted by all people on the basis of observation.

While many scholars capitulated to Kant's argument that God must be merely assumed, others, since the eighteenth century onward, have sought to reconstruct natural theology in a way that soundly refutes Kant and his critiques against the traditional arguments. But the biggest problem that Kant faces is this: his epistemology simply does not coincide with the Scriptures. Recall our discussion of Romans 1, where we looked at general revelation, natural theology, and Aquinas. Paul taught in Romans 1 that the eternal things of God, even his eternal power and deity, are clearly perceived through the things that are made by him. Paul is actually saying the opposite of Immanuel Kant. Paul argues that, to put it in Kantian terms, we *can* get from the phenomenal world to the noumenal world. He does not stop there, either. The inspired author goes on to say that, given God's general revelation of himself, he not only *can* be known, but *is* known through the created order, and that the knowledge of God is so clearly manifest in the world that the entire race of humanity is left with no excuse whatsoever for rejecting him. But if a wall exists, as Kant argues, between this world and the world where the idea of God resides, then plainly—and quite contradictory to Scripture—nonbelievers do indeed have an excuse for not giving their obedience and thanks to the Creator of heaven and earth. Kant has contended that, contrary to Paul, the things that are made by God do *not* clearly reveal his eternal power and divine nature. What we have at this point is an irreconcilable difference between the teachings of two men.

Kant and the Ontological Argument

One important feature of Kant's critique of the traditional arguments for God's existence was his contention that all of those arguments are reducible to or reliant upon the ontological argument, the argument that focuses on what it means *to be* "God." As such, Kant believed, the traditional arguments for God's existence are all invalid, because our experiences here cannot lead us to conclude anything certain about God. Briefly, the classic formulation of Anselm's ontological argument goes as follows: God is that-than-which-no-greater-can-be-thought, and he must, therefore, exist (i.e., he is *necessary*), for otherwise he would not be that-than-which-no-greater-can-be-thought. In other words, God alone is the greatest conceivable being in the universe. Which is greater: to exist as an idea in the mind only or to exist in reality? And if existence in reality is greater, which is greater: to exist necessarily or to exist unnecessarily? The point is this: since it is greater to exist than not, God must therefore exist, because, by definition, God is that-than-which-no-greater-can-be-thought.

Kant's objections to all the other traditional arguments centered on this ontological argument, because he saw that they all depend upon the concept of a necessary being (a being that *must* exist). Kant's challenge was this: the concept of necessary existence characterizes *thought,* not *reality.* That is to say, just because something can be shown to be *logically* necessary (using the intellect), does not mean that that something exists necessarily in the real world.

In any case, Kant contended that the ontological argument leaves the world of experience behind and speculates about the lofty world of ideas. For Kant, existence is never a necessary attribute; rather, existence is only an instance or occasion of something. For example, Kant argued that a dollar in his mind carried the exact same attributes as the one in his billfold. The only difference between the two was that one existed and the other did not. So, just because one can think of God's existing does not necessarily make his existing true. If reason demands that God exists, it does not necessitate his existence, because in the final analysis reality may be irrational. Just like Anselm's opponent Gaunilo, however, Kant missed the point entirely. Anselm responded that the ontological argument works in only *one* case, that is, for the existence of God. He was not discussing dollar bills or any other finite object. He was simply insisting that if God, the being than-which-no-greater-can-be-thought, can be thought of, then it is necessary that that being (God) exists.

SECTION IV

The Case for
God's Existence:
Four Possibilities

11

Illusion

Greek legend tells the story of a poor peasant named Gordius, who arrived into a public square of Phrygia (a region that Saint Paul traversed during his third missionary journey) on an oxcart. An ancient oracle had informed the people of that region that their future king would come riding into town on a wagon. Seeing Gordius on his oxcart, the people made him king, and in gratitude, Gordius dedicated his oxcart to Zeus and secured it to a post with a peculiar knot. Another oracle predicted that he who untied the knot would rule all of Asia. According to a later legend, Alexander the Great, who would eventually rule most of the civilized world, cut the knot with his sword. From that time onward, "cutting the Gordian knot" came to mean solving a difficult problem. Any Christian who wishes to engage the challenging task of apologetics has probably at times viewed his mission as just such a tangled knot.

As we have explored such preliminary issues as the basic principles of how we know what we know, our approach has intentionally not been exhaustive. At times, we have, at the risk of over-simplification, reduced the particulars so as to explain our apologetic task in the simplest possible way. We will continue in this manner now as we endeavor to prove the existence of God.

We are seeking to present an objective case for the existence of God. Our argument relies on a method first established by Augustine of Hippo. We will add to his method various insights from theologians and philosophers throughout history. Augustine's approach to arguing for the existence of God was to try to establish a *sufficient reason* to explain reality as we encounter it. A sufficient reason for the existence of God would be one that establishes his existence in such a way that logically demands that he exist, and that will rationally explain the existence of the universe and why it is the way it is. In other words, it will be a reason that requires nothing else for it to be the final, or necessary, reason that the world exists. A reason is sufficient if it is shown to be the only plausible explanation for something. Augustine approached this question through a process of elimination—by looking at possible theoretical explanations of reality. He would test them to see if they met or failed the tests of rationality.

In like manner, we will start our apologetic with the idea that there are four basic possibilities to explain reality. Each is independent of the others. If one of them is true, the others are false. The first possible explanation of reality (to be explored in this chapter) is that our experiences of reality are themselves an *illusion*. The second (in chapter 12) is that reality as we encounter it is *self-created*. Today, this explanation is expressed most often in terms of the universe's being the result of *chance* (see chapter 13). The third possibility is that reality is *self-existent*. The fourth is that the universe is *created* ultimately by something that is self-existent. We will consider these last two possibilities in chapters 14 and 15. Most apologists have had various nuances in their approaches to the question of God's existence. Most of their arguments do not explicitly use these terms or categories, but I firmly believe that any argument in the history of apologetics may be subsumed under these four generic categories. That is to say, all other forms of argument for or against the existence of God, or for explaining reality as we encounter it, can be included in one or more of these categories. So, to "cut the Gordian knot," as it were, our list of the possible explanations is generically exhaustive. Having tackled this particular problem of where to begin, we will now attempt to explain further our four categories.

Basically, we are endeavoring to argue that *if anything exists, God exists*. This is, of course, an extremely abbreviated form of the argument, and we have skipped over many steps in the process. But this is essentially what we will attempt to show: if anything exists, then something must exist necessarily. That is, something must exist that has the power of being within itself. In order to better understand "self-existence," consider the following: the reader (we assume) is holding a book. Let us also suppose, for the sake of argument, that the book is not a figment of our imagination, but that it exists in reality. We will try to prove such a statement later, but for now let us agree that the book exists. What we are saying about the book is one of four possible things: 1) the book is actually an illusion—it is not real; 2) the book has ultimately created itself; 3) the book has always existed from eternity past; or 4) the book has come into being ultimately through the work of a self-existent being. In order to give a sufficient reason for the book that the reader holds in his or her hands, one of our four possibilities must be true. The last two possibilities establish the existence of something that is self-existent; and if it is self-existent, it would also be eternal.

Many thinkers throughout history have argued that reality is an illusion. But by far the most popular alternative to explaining reality has been that the universe, or reality, is self-created (our second possibility). This view is posited today in opposition to divine creation. Many of the atheists we have discussed thus far fall back on some concept or other of a self-created universe. Seeing how this violates simple logic, others argue that the universe is eternal, that matter is eternal, and so on. At the very least, those who argue for a self-existent universe are arguing for an eternal something. We will attempt to determine whether that self-existent, eternal *something* is a personal or an impersonal something. Our hope at this point will be to show that both reason and science demand the existence of a self-existent, eternal being to account for the existence of anything else. But our hope for the end of this discussion is that we will have shown the character of that self-existent something to be a personal being, whom we call God.

The Testimony of René Descartes

It may seem a waste of time to expend any effort in eliminating the first alternative, that everything that we think exists is but an illusion; but serious philosophers have argued precisely that point—that the world and everything in it is simply somebody else's dream and does not exist at all. To deal with this first alternative, I shall call as my primary witness René Descartes (1596–1650), the father of modern rationalism, a seventeenth-century thinker who was also a mathematician. Descartes was very much concerned about a new form of skepticism that had arrived on the scene of Western Europe following the sixteenth-century Protestant Reformation.

There had arisen, in the wake of the Protestant Reformation, a crisis in authority. Previous to the Reformation, if Christians had disputes, they could appeal to the monolithic church of Rome to render a verdict. When the church gave the verdict, that settled the controversy, because the authority of the church was deemed to be at least sacrosanct, and at best, infallible. With the challenge to the authority of the church that came with the Protestant Reformation, the whole question of "How can we know anything for sure?" became a serious problem. Not only did people see the breakdown of church authority but they also witnessed the breakdown and collapse of scientific authority. In addition to the Protestant Reformation, the sixteenth century saw a scientific revolution—the so-called "Copernican revolution" in astronomy. Copernicus raised all kinds of questions about the trustworthiness of science.

This controversy over the Copernican revolution carried over into the seventeenth century when the Galileo episode became prominent in the life of the church. Galileo with his telescope was confirming the mathematical theories of sixteenth-century astronomers. So not only in theology and philosophy but also in science there was a crisis of authority. Descartes was trying, in his philosophical inquiry, to reestablish some foundation for certainty with respect to truth. He was looking for what he called "clear and distinct" ideas—ideas that were indubitable, ideas that could not be rejected without rejecting reason at the same time— which ideas could then form a foundation for the reconstruction of knowledge, whether in the scientific sphere or in the theological, philosophical arena.

The process Descartes followed in order to achieve such *certainty* was a process of *uncertainty,* or of skepticism. He embarked upon a rigorous pursuit of skepticism, in which he sought to bring doubt upon everything he could conceivably doubt. He wanted to give the second glance to every assumed truth that people held. He kept asking, "Do we really know that this is true?"

I sometimes follow such a method myself. I'll make a list and say to myself, "What are ten things that I know for sure?" I'll write them down and then subject those ten things to the most rigorous criticism I can, to make sure that I'm not just believing them because somebody I like taught them to me or because of my traditions, or the subculture I come from. I want to know, "How do I know that these things that I think are true really are true?"

Such a process of questioning is one of the most important principles for breakthroughs in any kind of knowledge. It is how philosophers, musicians, and scientists break through to new views. They challenge assumptions that previous generations made and accepted and passed on. The Ptolemaic system of astronomy survived for more than a thousand years simply because people accepted theories without the theories ever having been proved. We need to subject our own thinking to a rigorous cross-examination. We have all seen what happens in court trials: we hear one side of a case, and it makes sense. We're sitting there nodding, "Yes, yes, yes," until the cross-examination comes, and people begin to raise questions about the testimony that we've heard. By the time we're done listening to both sides, we're not so sure who's telling the truth.

This doesn't mean we surrender to skepticism. Critical analysis and skepticism are not the same thing. Descartes was engaged in rigorous critical analysis. He said, "I'm going to doubt everything I can conceivably doubt. I'm going to doubt what I see with my eyes and what I hear with my ears because I understand that my senses can be deceived." Centuries before, Augustine spoke of the problem of the "bent oar." When we place an oar in the water, it appears to the naked eye that it *bends,* when in fact it remains straight. Descartes said, "Maybe this world is controlled by the great deceiver, the great satanic, demonic being, who is a liar, who constantly gives me a false view of reality. Maybe he keeps bringing these illusions in front of me to deceive me. How can I know that reality is as I perceive it to be?"

Remember the four basic principles we started with (chapters 3-8), one of which was the basic reliability of sense perception. We spoke of the "basic" reliability of senses because we know our senses are not perfect. They can mislead us. This is what is known as the subject-object problem. How do I know that the objective world out there is as I perceive it from within my own subjective perspective? Descartes was acutely conscious of that problem, so he came up with some of the most preposterous possibilities. He said, "Now, maybe it doesn't make a lot of sense to think of a great deceiver producing this vast illusion out there, but it is possible. And if it is possible, then I cannot know for sure that reality is as I perceive it to be. So what can I know for sure?"

"I Think, Therefore I Am Not an Illusion!"

Having gone through this systematic doubting process, Descartes came to the conclusion for which he is so well known: *Cogito ergo sum.* "I think, therefore, I am." He said, in essence, "No matter how skeptical I become, the one thing that I cannot doubt, whenever I'm doubting whatever it is that I'm doubting, is that I *am* doubting. There's no way I can escape the reality of doubt."

Then Descartes raised this question: "What is required for there to be doubt?" He argued that for there to be doubt, there must be cognition. Doubt requires thought—conscious thought—because doubt is an action of thinking. Without thinking, there can be no doubting. So if I'm doubting, I know that I'm thinking. At least I *think* that I'm thinking. And if I say I don't think that I'm thinking? Well, in order for me to say I don't think that I'm thinking, I must be thinking. I can't escape the reality that I am thinking, because to doubt is to think. And then he goes to the next premise: "Just as doubt requires a doubter, just as thought requires a thinker, if *I* am doubting, I must conclude, rationally, that *I* am thinking; and if *I* am thinking, then I must *be*. I must exist, because that which does not exist cannot think, that which cannot think cannot doubt; and since there's no doubt that I'm doubting, it would mean also that I'm thinking; and if I'm thinking, I am also existing." And so he came to the conclusion, "*Cogito*—I'm thinking—*ergo*—therefore—*sum*—I am."

People who are not students of philosophy may look at the elaborate process that Descartes went through and say, "This is why philosophy is so foolish, that somebody would spend all this time and all this effort to learn what everybody who is alive and awake and conscious already knows—that they are, in fact, existing. Nobody really is denying their own existence. They're not really believing that they are simply an actor appearing in somebody else's dream." But again, remember what Descartes was about. He was a mathematician, and he was looking for certainty in the philosophical realm that would equal in force and power and rational compulsion the certainty that can be arrived at in mathematics.

The reason this is important is that Descartes is disposing with the first option—that reality is an illusion. There may indeed be illusions in reality, but if we say that *all* reality is an illusion, that would mean that nothing exists, including myself; and, as Descartes has shown, I can never doubt the existence of myself without proving the reality of myself. The first of the four alternatives, as a sufficient explanation for the universe, has to be discarded because Descartes' argument proves that *something* exists; and that something that exists, if nothing else, is his own consciousness.

I have argued that if my piece of chalk exists, it would ultimately prove the existence of God. Yet I acknowledge that my chalk could be an illusion. But even if it is an illusion, there must be someone suffering the illusion. Just as doubt requires a doubter, so illusions require something experiencing the illusions. Thus the presence of an illusion proves that something exists. If something exists (either the chalk or the thinking self) that something would ultimately demand the existence of God. For my apologetic to work I must establish that *something* exists. I thank Descartes for solving that problem for me—by proving the existence of himself.

There are philosophers who don't agree with Descartes's conclusion that *cogito ergo sum*. They insist that there's no basis in reality for coming to that conclusion. And they point out correctly, at least this far, that Descartes made two major assumptions along the way in order to come to his conclusion.

Descartes's first assumption is the law of noncontradiction. He assumed logic. He assumed rationality. He said, "If there is doubt in my mind, then I must be doubting." That is a logical conclusion based upon the law of noncontradiction. The existential irrationalist may say, "Well, he could still be living in an illusion where doubters can doubt without doubting." But remember that classical apologetics is only trying to show that *reason* requires the existence of a self-existent eternal being. If somebody is an atheist and says, "I don't believe in the existence of God because I don't believe in rationality," I give them the microphone and say, "Please tell the whole world that your alternative to theism is absurd. Save me the difficulty of having to demonstrate it." They have taken themselves out of any intelligent discussion as soon as they admit that their premise is one of irrationality. Descartes was saying that, just as mathematics is rational, just as sound science is rational, so sound philosophy must also be rational; and if we are going to be rational and if we are going to be logical, we cannot deny that to doubt we must think, and to think we must exist.

The second premise Descartes is assuming is the second principle that we considered earlier, the law of causality. When Descartes says that doubting requires a doubter, he is saying that doubt is an effect that requires a cause. Some of Descartes' critics would say, "No, this doesn't prove that Descartes exists, because he's assuming logic, and he's assuming causality, and we don't accept those premises." And we reply, "That's fine, if we want to be irrational," because we saw that the law of causality is simply an extension of the law of noncontradiction; we saw that the law of causality, which says that every effect must have a cause, is a *formal* truth. It is as formally true as two plus two equals four, because it is true by definition. We said at the beginning that we dare not negotiate the law of noncontradiction and we dare not negotiate the law of causality, because if we do, we'll end up in absurdity. But if we use these principles that are necessary for all intelligible discourse in all science, in all philosophy, in all theology, then we cannot escape the conclusion that Descartes gives. We can, through a resistless logic, *through formal reasoning alone,* come to the conclusion of our own existence. We can then eliminate illusion as a sufficient grounds for disproving the existence of the world.

12

SELF-CREATION

The second possible explanation for reality is by far the most frequent alternative proffered by opponents of theism. Rarely do atheists speak plainly about the universe being strictly "self-created," but many theories that pass for viable accounts of the universe are nothing more than arguments for self-creation. It is indeed rare that opponents of theism use the phrase "self-created," because of its manifest absurdity. Rather they mask the absurdity by using terminology that is not so self-evidently absurd. They will use concepts such as "chance creation" or "spontaneous generation."

Self-Creation Is Analytically False

Before we look at the variations of this second possibility, we shall take a moment to discuss the idea itself. Self-creation is a concept that is, in philosophical language, *analytically false*. Recall our discussion about the law of causality, and how the statement "Every effect must have a cause" is a "formal" or "analytical" truth, which means simply that it is true *by definition*. Having analyzed the words within the statement and their relationship to each other, if it is then clear by its very definition that it is true, we know that it is analytically true. The idea of self-creation, when examined in this fashion, shows itself to be false *by definition*.

When we looked at the law of noncontradiction, we noted

that the law itself has no content, that is, the law does not tell us *what* to think but *how* to think. As such, it is a tool of logic that we can apply to the *idea* of a self-created universe. In order to affirm a self-created universe, one must reject the law of non-contradiction. Plainly, the second possibility of explaining the universe—that it is self-created—is self-referentially absurd. For something to create itself, or to be its own effect as well as its own cause, it would have to exist before it existed. The universe, to be self-created, would have to be before it was. Stated in terms of the law of noncontradiction, the universe would have to be and not be at the same time and in the same relationship. Imagine if Hamlet had rejected the law of noncontradiction: "To be *and* not to be. That is the question." That, of course, is no question at all; that is absurd. Self-creation is, *by definition,* analytically false. We set out, as Augustine did, to entertain certain possibilities long enough to ascertain whether or not they pass the tests of rationality. This one cannot even get off the ground. But before we leave it, we will look at some of the ways this concept has been articulated.

Self-Creation vs. Self-Existence

First, however, let us consider the sharp difference between self-creation and the concept of *self-existence.* To say that something is self-existent is to say that it is eternal and has the power of being within itself—it is uncreated. There is nothing absurd or irrational in the idea of self-existence or eternal existence. As we will see later in more detail, self-existence is a rational *possibility* because it violates no law of reason. It violates no law of logic to speak of something's being self-existent. To speak of its being self-created, on the other hand, does violate rationality and the laws of logic because it violates the law of noncontradiction. Nothing can be self-created, not even God.

Two boys were arguing about the origin of things. One of them said to the other, "Where did the trees come from?"

The second boy said, "God made the trees."

"Where did the grass come from?"

"God made the grass."

"Well, where did you come from?"

"God made me."

"Well, then, where did God come from?"

And the profound answer the little boy gave was that, "God made himself."

The answer may be cute, but it is not sound. Even God could not make himself, because that would mean that he would have to be before he was. He would have to be and not be at the same time and in the same way. Not even God has the ability to be and not be at the same time and in the same relationship. Hamlet understood the options: "To be or not to be." We can't have it both ways at the same time and in the same relationship.

Varieties of Self-Creation

Self-creation has been advocated in various ways. One of the most widespread attempts to use the concept of self-creation as a substitute for creation of the universe by a self-existent, eternal being took place during the Enlightenment. Some, though certainly not all, Enlightenment thinkers were atheists. Some of those who were atheists sought to replace the concept of a creator God with the concept of "spontaneous generation." Spontaneous generation means that things simply begin on their own, without any cause. This, of course, ignores the fundamental law of science that *ex nihilo nihil fit* ("out of nothing, nothing comes"). Nothing does not produce something, because nothing *cannot* produce something.

I remember as a young person in high school, listening to our science teachers belittle these ideas and tell us that nobody believed in spontaneous generation anymore. Of course the notion of spontaneous generation *should* have been debunked the minute it was uttered because it involved a logical impossibility from the outset. But to my astonishment, some years later, I read an essay by a Nobel Prize–winning scientist from the West Coast on this concept of spontaneous generation. He said, "We have come to the place now in modern science where we can no longer affirm the concept of spontaneous generation." But then he went on to say that, "reality cannot be generated by itself spontaneously, and we have to replace that concept of spontaneous generation with a more refined and sophisticated scientific idea," which he defined as, "gradual spontaneous generation." As I read that, I laughed, thinking, "This man holds a Nobel Prize in science. This is a very learned man, and he's talking nonsense like this! 'Gradual spontaneous generation.' In other words, we can't get something out of nothing quickly; it takes time! You have to wait, in the evolutionary process, for this nothing to yield something. It may take eons and eons, but if you have enough patience, sooner or later, something can create itself!" At this point, the philosopher and the scientist butt heads, because the scientist has left half of the scientific method back in the laboratory.

More recently, I encountered a second variation of the idea of self-creation. The day that the Hubble spacecraft was launched, there was a radio broadcast in which a prominent astrophysicist was quoted regarding the significance of "now increasing our understanding of outer space and changing the horizons by virtue of this new technology." He went on to explain how the beginnings of the universe took place, in his judgment, 15 to 18 billion years ago, "when the universe exploded into being." Here the astrophysicist was using language heavily conditioned by philosophy: the word *being* is filled with philosophical content. And he talked about the origin of the universe; he put a time frame on it: 15 to 18 billion years ago the universe "exploded" into being. Now, he didn't say the universe exploded into its *present form,* which would be one thing. It is one thing to say that the universe was in one form—that it existed, that it was real, that it had substance, and then it changed dramatically with the Big Bang. But this physicist said it exploded into "being." I thought, "What do you mean, exploded into being? What was it before the explosion? Was it the opposite of being, the antithesis of being, which in philosophical categories is non-being, which is a synonym for nothing?"

The notion that reality comes into being by way of a great explosion is philosophical nonsense. It is sheer irrationality. I suspect that if I had had the opportunity to interview the physicist who made that statement, he would be quick to say, "I misspoke. I meant to say that there was a present or previous state of being that changed at the time of the great explosion, but I don't mean to suggest that the explosion came from nothing into something." I hope and trust that that's what the physicist would have said.

We see spontaneous generation, "gradual" spontaneous generation, and universes exploding into being. But far and away the most frequent form of self-creation that we meet in the modern culture is the idea of creation by chance, namely, that the universe comes into being through some *power* attributed to chance. Usually the formula goes, space plus time plus chance. I've written a whole book on this idea, entitled *Not a Chance.*[1] This idea is tied to modern concepts of quantum mechanics and physics, which theories tend to teach that, at the subatomic level, we have scientific evidence of things coming into being out of nothing. We'll look at that idea more closely in our next chapter.

The oldest question in philosophy and in science is, "Why is there something rather than nothing?" If there ever was a time when there was nothing—no God, no matter, no nothing—what could there possibly be now? If there ever was a time when there was absolutely nothing, the only way you could explain the presence of something would be through some kind of self-creation, something coming out of nothing by itself. That is a task I would not assign to God, to gremlins, to a scientist, to an amino acid, or to anything else.

13

CREATION BY CHANCE

I mentioned in passing that I had written an entire book (*Not a Chance*) on the subject of chance creation. What provoked the writing of that book was my having read several offerings from people in the scientific community trying to explain some of the most difficult concepts for the modern scientist to deal with—things that occur in the laboratory with respect to experiments, with respect to subatomic particles and light and quantum mechanics. As I point out in that book, I am neither a physicist nor an expert in quantum physics. I do not presume to correct physicists on what they are learning in their experimentation, nor am I trying to put up barriers to those experiments as they seek to expand their understanding of reality. My problem with the physicists was not their experimentation but their articulation of the results of their experiments and the inferences they were drawing from the data they worked with.

I don't have to be a physicist to be able to analyze the content, significance, and coherency of statements and propositions. That is something that philosophers major in—giving a logical analysis of the truth-value of propositions. When physicists articulate their theories in ways that are linguistically nonsense, then it is time for the philosopher to blow the whistle and say, "We don't understand what you're saying because what you're saying is unintelligible."

In the first chapter of *Not a Chance,* I wrote that the mere existence of chance is enough to rip God from his cosmic throne. Chance leaves God out of a job. My basic thesis in the book was that there is no such thing as chance. The greatest myth in modern mythology is the *myth of chance.*

Coin Tosses and "Chance" Encounters

One thing that led me to write *Not a Chance* was a discussion I had with a professor of the philosophy of science in the graduate school at Harvard. We were discussing the origin of the universe. He denied Creation, and I asked him, "Where did the universe come from?"

He said, "The universe was created by chance."

I looked at him and repeated his assertion: "The world was created by chance?"

He said, "Yes."

At that point I reached into my pocket and took out a quarter. I flipped it in the air, caught it, and turned it over. The heads side was up. I said, "Now, I just tossed that coin in the air. What were the chances that that coin, given that it didn't stand on its end, would come up either heads or tails?"

He said, "A hundred percent, because it only has two options—either heads or tails."

I said, "Okay, mathematically, what are the odds that it comes up heads?"

He said, "Fifty-fifty."

I said, "Good. Now let me ask you this: How much influence does *chance* have on whether it turns up heads or tails? In other words, if we had a completely controlled experiment where we had a coin on an armature of some sort, and it was started heads up every single time, and the experiment took place in a vacuum, where exactly the same amount of force was exercised on that coin every single time, and it went exactly the same height in the vacuum every single time, and had the same number of revolutions in the vacuum every single time, and landed at the same place every single time, and we didn't have the variables of whether you were going to turn it over, catch it here, here, here, or here, or any of those variables, would you be able to increase to more than fifty-fifty the percentages of its coming up heads?"

He said, "Of course."

I said, "Right," because we both understood that the causal agencies involved in the coin's coming up either heads or tails have nothing to do with some mythological power called chance. They have to do with the factors I've mentioned—whether you start it heads up or tails up, how much force is exerted by the thumb, how dense the atmosphere is, how high it goes, how many revolutions it makes, and so forth. All of those variables can impact the outcome of the experiment. But we know that, given all those variables that we don't have time to examine every time, the coin has to come up one of two ways, heads or tails, and so we say the odds are fifty-fifty.

Now, there's nothing at all wrong with the word *chance*. It is a perfectly meaningful word when we use it to describe mathematical possibilities. It becomes a synonym for "the odds." What are the odds that something will happen? What are the chances that something will happen? We even, in a popular way, make meaningful use of the term *chance* when we speak of "chance encounters."

Once when traveling by train from Orlando to California, I had an eight-hour layover in Chicago. I got off the train in the morning at the time the commuter trains were coming into downtown Chicago from the suburbs. It just so happened that I boarded the train late in the afternoon at the same time that the commuter trains were going back to their destinations. When I got off the train in Chicago in the morning, I was walking through the building, crowded with a teeming mass of humanity, and I looked up and saw a friend, Al, whom I hadn't seen in ten years. We had a wonderful conversation. Eight hours later I came back into the same terminal building. Again there were thousands of people crowding their way to the trains. And again I ran into Al! What are the odds of that?

When I left Florida on that trip, I did not design, plan, or intend to meet Al in the corridors of the station there in Chicago. When he left his home that morning, he had no intention of meeting me; we bumped into each other in a "chance encounter." But chance doesn't explain *why* it happened. That is to say, chance didn't *cause* our encounter. The reason we met each other is that we happened to be at the same place at the same time for a host of different reasons that converged in time and space.

Can Chance Actually Cause Anything?

Chance is a perfectly legitimate word for describing coin tosses and unexpected encounters. Today, however, the word *chance* has been subtly elevated to indicate something far more than mathematical odds or probabilities. To many modern minds, chance is seen as having *causal power*. I asked my friend at Harvard, "Do you see with my coin-toss analogy that there was no power being enacted or exercised, by this thing you call chance, to cause the coin to come up heads?" He agreed that this was so. In fact, he literally took the heel of his right hand and banged himself in the head, saying, "I guess I shouldn't have said that the universe was created by chance."

The *ontological status* of chance is *zero*. Chance has no *being*. Chance is not a *thing* that operates and works upon other things. It is simply a mental concept that refers to mathematical possibilities, but that in and of itself has no ontology. It has no being.

A piece of chalk has some being to it. Physicists and philosophers can stay busily engaged for centuries trying to penetrate the ultimate essence of a piece of chalk, but one thing we will agree on is that the chalk is not nothing—a piece of chalk is something. It has ontological status; it is a thing. It has existence. It is real, rather than an illusion. Likewise, I have ontological status. I am a being. I'm not the supreme being, I'm not a divine being, I'm only a human being, but I *am* something rather than nothing. But when we come to "chance," we are talking about something that has no being; and because it has no being, it has no power—

because that which is absent of being must, of necessity, also be absent of power. For power to exist or to operate, it must be the power of *something.* We can't have power being generated by *nothing* anymore than we can have objects being generated by nothing. Power or doing requires a doer, just as Descartes said that thought requires a thinker.

Philosophers and scientists down through the ages have understood that the word *chance* is a word that defines our ignorance. We throw the word *chance* into the equation when we don't know what's going on out there. When we can't do our homework analytically and come up to a cogent understanding, we begin to attribute things to chance, to the *power* of chance. We play games of chance where the cards are shuffled randomly, and when the cards are dealt, there are statistical odds that we can determine on the basis of how they were dealt. I like to play cards. I've studied mathematical possibilities in bridge and gin rummy. I play according to the odds, and it really helps me to know what the mathematical possibilities are in so-called games of chance. But it is still a game of chance, because I don't know how the cards were sorted. The reason why I am dealt the hand that I am dealt in a game of bridge or in a game of gin rummy is found in how they were arranged when they were shuffled the first time, how they were arranged when they were shuffled the second time, how they were dealt, and in what sequence they were dealt. There was no invisible demon called chance that jumped into the card dealer and caused certain cards to be dealt in a certain sequence. Chance has no being. And since it has no being, it has no power.

So I said again to my Harvard friend, "Chance is not a thing that can exercise power. Do you agree?"

And finally he said, "Yes, chance is not a thing."

Now let me say it a little differently. Chance is no-thing. Chance is nothing, and when we say that the universe was created by chance, we are saying, analytically, that the universe was created by nothing. We're not just attributing some insignificant power to chance; we're attributing the supreme power to chance by declaring it possible, by chance, not only to do something, but to bring into being the whole of reality. That concept, under five minutes of analysis, yields its own absurdity and manifests itself as the worst kind of mythology. But if we couch it in respectable language and communicate it in the terminology of science, it becomes like alchemy, where people think they can turn metal into gold. The myth of alchemy was couched in scientific jargon and was respected for centuries. We can give respectability to mythology if we couch our myths in sufficiently academic language. But no matter how we slice it, if we attribute any power to chance, we're talking nonsense because chance is nothing. If we think it's something, then we must ask, what is it? How much does it weigh? Is it an energy field? Is it electromagnetism? What is the genesis of this power? When we say that something is "chance," we are simply saying, "We don't know."

I recall again those writings and discussions on science that led me to write *Not a Chance*. It is one thing to say, "I do not know why these subatomic particles behave the way they do, or why none of our scientific paradigms can explain this behavior. I know that it is happening. I'm observing it. I'm experimenting with it. I just don't know why it happens." At that point, the scientist is exercising a proper demeanor for scientific investigation. When he bumps up to the limit of his knowledge, he says, "I don't know." That should be done in biology, in chemistry, in physics, in philosophy, and in theology. That should be the mark of any authentic investigator of truth. It is one thing to say, "I don't know," but quite another to say, "*Nothing* is producing this effect." In order to know that nothing is producing something, we would have to know every conceivable possible force that exists in or outside of the universe. Only omniscience would give us that kind of knowledge. I think, as a matter of prudence, we ought to stop saying that nothing causes something, because it's a nonsense statement. It's not just bad theology, it's bad science, to advocate self-creation under any name.

14

A SELF-EXISTENT BEING

We have been examining the various options for explaining reality as we encounter it. Can we find a "sufficient reason" to account for the world we live in? We have looked at the first option, that reality is an illusion, and have eliminated that possibility. The second possibility we looked at was that reality is self-created, or that is was created by chance. We saw that, from an analytical perspective, this is a self-defeating idea. It is absurd by definition because it is rationally impossible.

We will now consider the final two alternatives: that reality is self-existent, or that reality has been created by something that is self-existent. In this chapter, we will consider these two options in terms of a self-existent *being*; in chapter 15 we will consider the possibility that *the universe itself* is self-existent.

By now we have established that there must be something, somewhere, somehow that is self-existent, because we have eliminated (in chapters 11-13) the other two possibilities. Now we have to decide what, precisely, is self-existent. But first we must look at the concept of self-existence. The first thing we ask is, "Is it possible for anything actually to be self-existent?" We have seen that it is logically impossible for something to be self-*created*, because for something to create itself, it would have to exist before it was, and it would therefore have to be and not be at the same time and in the same relationship. Logic eliminates this as a rational possibility.

Now we face the question, "Is the idea of something being self-existent and *eternal* (rather than self-created) a rational possibility?" When we put side-by-side the two ideas, self-creation and self-existence, they seem very similar. But here is the difference: there is nothing illogical, whatsoever, about the idea of a self-existent, eternal being—that is, of a being not caused by something else. We said earlier that one of the problems we encounter when discussing the existence of God is that some people misunderstand the idea of the law of cause and effect, saying it means that *everything* must have a cause. But the law of causality says only that every *effect* must have a cause, because an effect by definition is that which has been produced by something outside of itself. But the idea of an *uncaused being* is perfectly rational.

Of course, the mere fact that we can conceive of an uncaused being—something that exists in and of itself from all eternity and that is not caused by something outside of itself—does not mean that such a being would indeed have to be. The present point is simply that we can *conceive of* the idea of a self-existent eternal being without violating rationality. Reason allows for the *possibility* of self-existence, while it does not allow for the possibility of self-creation.

In fact, as we shall see, once we conclude that something does exist, rather than everything being an illusion, then the idea of a self-existent being becomes not only possible but *necessary*.

The idea of self-existence, which in theology we call the attribute of aseity, is the idea that something exists in and of itself; it is *uncaused, uncreated,* and differs from everything in the universe that has a cause. A self-existent, eternal being is one that has the power to be, in and of itself. It doesn't receive its existence or its being from something antecedent to itself. It has its existence inherently. And because it has its existence inherently, it has it eternally. There was never a time when this self-existent being did not exist. If there were a time when this self-existent being did not exist, then it would not be self-existent; it would have to have been created by something else. A self-existent being is, by definition, one that always has been.

We Need a Self-Existent Being

As we look more closely at the idea of self-existence, we see that it is not only possible from a viewpoint of reason but also necessary. When Thomas Aquinas argued for the existence of God, one of his five arguments was from the principle of "necessary being." In theology, God has been called the *ens necessarium*—that being whose being is *necessary*.

There are two distinct ways in which philosophers describe God as a necessary being. The first is that he is necessary by virtue of rationality; if anything exists, the existence of God is *rationally* necessary. If something exists *now*, reason demands that something has *always* existed—that something, somewhere has the power of being within itself—or we simply could not account for the existence of anything. If there were ever a time when there was nothing, absolutely nothing, what could there possibly be now, except nothing? *Ex nihilo nihil fit*—"out of nothing, nothing can come"—unless something comes by itself, creating itself, which, as we have seen, is a rational impossibility.

We know that something exists now. That means that there could never have been a time when there was absolutely nothing. There has always had to be something. So far we have not demonstrated that that something is God; we're only arguing at this point that there must be something that has the power of being within itself and that has always been there. And because that is a being whose being is necessary logically, it is a logical necessity that we postulate such an idea of self-existent being.

We began with the rational *possibility* of a self-existent being, but given the thesis that there is *something* that exists now, rather than *nothing*, that takes us to the next step: there must be a self-existent being through rational *necessity*. When we talk about God being a necessary being, in the first instance what we mean is that his existence is a rational necessity. Reason demands the existence of a self-existent, eternal being. That is very important for the Christian who is trying to defend his faith, because the guns of criticism against Judeo-Christianity are aimed almost exclusively at the idea of Creation and the idea of a Creator. If one can get rid of Creation and a Creator, then the whole concept of God collapses. So people are trying to argue that if you are going to be rational and scientific, then you have to believe in a universe without God. What we're trying to do is turn the guns around and say that such people need to realize that what they are postulating as an alternative to full-bodied theism is manifest irrationality and absurdity—that reason demands there be a necessary being.

This necessary being is rationally necessary. He is also *ontologically* necessary. Here it gets a bit more abstract, a little more difficult, for those who are not students of philosophy. I have already defined this term *ontology,* but we need to take the time to go over it again. Ontology is the study or the science of being. When we say that God is ontologically necessary, we mean that he exists by the necessity of his own being. He doesn't exist merely because reason says he has to exist; he exists eternally because he has the power of being, in himself, in such a way that his being cannot *not* be. That is the difference between us and God. We say that God is the supreme being and we say that we are human beings, but the difference between the supreme being and the human being is *being.* My being or existence is creaturely existence. I am a dependent, derived, contingent creature. I cannot sustain myself forever. There was a time when I was not. There will be a time when my life and the form in which I am living it now will undergo some kind of transition. I will, in fact, die. Right now, for me to continue to exist in my present state, I need water, oxygen, a heartbeat, brainwaves, and so on. I am dependent upon all of these things in order to continue to exist. A hundred years ago there was no R. C. Sproul. I did not exist. Now I exist. I have a beginning in time, and my life can be measured in terms of time. The whole process of my life involves constant generation and decay, change and mutation. This is the supreme character-istic of contingent beings, or creatures; they change constantly. That which has self-existent, eternal being is changeless, because it is never losing any of the power of its being, nor is it gaining anything in the scope of its being. It is what it is, eternally. It has being, itself, within its own power. That is what we mean by a self-existent, eternal being, whose being is ontologically necessary; that is, it cannot help but be. Pure being is dependent upon noth-ing for its continuity of existence or its origin of existence; it is not in a state of becoming, as Plato understood. It is in a state of pure being, and pure being cannot *not* be.

Is the God of the Bible a Self-Existent Being?

We must now consider the link between the notion of self-existence and biblical theism. For this is how God revealed himself with his sacred name to Moses in the Midianite wilder-ness. Moses watched this bush that was burning but was not being consumed, and he heard this voice speaking to him out of the bush, calling him by name, saying, "Moses, Moses! . . . take your sandals off your feet, for the place on which you are standing is holy ground" (Ex. 3:4, 5). Moses then asked God the big question: "Who are you?" And God answered by giving his sacred name, the name by which he is known from all genera-tions: "I AM WHO I AM" (v. 14). Not "I was" or "I will be" or "I'm in the process of change or becoming," but, "I AM WHO I AM." He uses the verb "to be" in the present tense. This is the name of God, the one whose being is always present, eternally present, and eternally unchanging, without whose being nothing else could possibly be.

15

A Self-Existent Universe

We have been looking at the four alternatives for explaining reality. We looked, first of all, at the possibility that everything is an illusion, and borrowing heavily from the arguments of Descartes we eliminated that option. We looked at various theories of self-creation, all of which collapse by their own weight because they are, at their center, irrational. Then we noticed that the two remaining possibilities both contain the idea of self-existence. In our last study, I pointed out that if something exists now, the idea of something that is self-existent is not only possible but rationally necessary. Then I made the distinction between that which is rationally necessary and that which is ontologically necessary. Whatever this self-existent, eternal something is, it must be not only rationally necessary but ontologically necessary as well. And that squares with the Judeo-Christian understanding of the nature of God. However, there are those who agree that *something* must be self-existent and eternal but they argue that the self-existent, eternal something is the *universe* and not God.

Scientific paradigms change. In my own lifetime, we saw the advent of the Big Bang theory of the origin of the universe, which was not accepted when I was a high school student but now has pretty much won the day. In simple terms, the Big Bang theory is that there was a time 15 to 18 billion years ago, give or take a few billion, when all that existed was what is described by some as a

"point of singularity." This point of singularity involved the compaction of all matter and all energy in the universe. That is, all of
the stuff of reality, at least in its nascent form, was compressed
into this infinitesimal point of singularity. This point of singularity existed from all eternity in a state of organization—that is, it
was compacted in a steady, organized, stable way. And then at
some point, 15 to 18 billion years ago, this point of singularity,
for reasons unknown to us, exploded, and out of that explosion
came the material universe as we know it today.

Since that great explosion, the universe now is in a state where
everything is moving from organization to disorganization, just
as when something explodes and things move out from the center, away from their point of compaction or condensation into a
state of disorganization.

That raises all kinds of questions. The first question is this: If
the universe is moving toward disorganization, how did it become
organized in the first place? For if it is moving toward disorganization, then it is moving *from* organization.

The other law we have to wrestle with when considering the
Big Bang theory is the law of inertia. The law of inertia teaches
that things in motion tend to remain in motion unless acted upon
by an outside force, and things that are at rest tend to remain at
rest unless acted upon by an outside force. For example, this law
of inertia is what makes golf so difficult and yet what makes golf
possible. The golf ball begins at rest; it is placed upon the tee.
And the golfer himself is at rest. Then he walks up to the ball and
the first thing he does is address the ball. He says, "Good morning, ball." Then he takes his club and swings it. He sets the club
in motion. And that which is in motion hits that which is at rest
and propels it down the fairway. But while the ball is moving, it
is finding resistance from various forces of nature until it lands on
the ground. And once it lands, it won't roll forever because the
friction of the ground impedes its continued progress. Finally, the
ball comes to rest again.

Now, fortunately, there are these outside forces working

against our efforts to keep the golf ball in motion. Because if there were no outside forces, and we set the golf ball in motion, the drive would go forever, and that would be the end of the game. We would lose the ball and there would be no way of scoring the game. The outside forces, even though they are frustrating our efforts to hit the ball farther, nevertheless also make it possible for the game of golf to be played.

What Caused the Big Bang?

A thing at rest tends to remain at rest unless some *outside force* is applied to it. And once it begins moving, it is going to stay moving unless its motion is retarded by some other outside force. Now the sixty-four million dollar question about the Big Bang is, What caused the bang? What outside force caused it to happen? Some people say we don't need to answer that question, because the answer goes beyond science and into the realm of philosophy or theology or religion or whatever. I say, "Wait a minute! When we are going to give an explanation for all of reality, and you pin all of our hopes upon this concept of a Big Bang, why don't we answer the question, What caused the Big Bang?" Scientific theory is innately concerned with matters of causality, and this is the big question of causality: What caused the Big Bang? It is a cop-out, academically and intellectually, to say, "I'm not going to go there." If you are going to postulate a thesis for the origin of everything, then you are begging the question, What is the outside force that causes this monumental change in our little point of singularity—that causes it to move, to cause reality to change from the state of organization toward disorganization?

Biblical Christianity has the answer to that question. Christianity's answer is the doctrine of Creation: we have a self-existent, eternal being who has the power of motion, who has the ability to move that which is not moving. That is what Aristotle understood when he talked about the "unmoved mover." He understood that there has to be an origin to motion, and that that which has the origin of motion must have the power of motion

within itself, just as it must have the power of being within itself.
And that is why we assign these attributes to God.

Is Matter Itself Eternal?

But is it possible that this matter that is compacted in the Big Bang
point of singularity is *itself* the self-existent, eternal being? This
is what materialism assumes: the universe itself is not merely 15
to 18 billion years old; the present *motion* of the universe goes
back to that point in time, but the actual ingredients of reality are
eternal. In response to this line of reasoning I would ask, "What
is it in the universe that is eternal? Is it the piece of chalk that I
use in my lectures? Is it my car keys? Is it the sun? Is it me, as a
person?"

And of course the materialist will say, "Don't be ridiculous.
You know that those are all either manufactured things or things
that otherwise came into being that previously did not exist. No,
we're not saying that the sun is eternal; we're not saying that you
are eternal; we're not saying that the chalk is eternal or that the
car keys are eternal. We know that the chief characteristic of matter is its *mutability*— it changes, and it changes from one state
into another state so that it is not stable, eternally, and therefore
it is in *process;* it is in a state of *becoming* and not in a state of
pure being. Anything that we find within the universe is changing; it manifests contingency, it is dependent on or derived from
something else. These things cannot be the ultimate core of being
of the universe that we are describing in terms of a self-existent,
eternal something."

But then the materialist will go on to explain, "Okay, we
grant that this eraser or this piece of chalk is not the eternal reality that is self-existent, but it is *made up of* elements that are
generated by a self-existent, eternal something. This self-existent,
eternal something, contrary to religion, is not transcendent; it is
immanent. That is, we don't have to appeal to something above
and beyond this universe to account for this universe."

The Christian replies that outside of the whole realm of the creaturely universe stands this self-existent, eternal being that we call God, who is the Creator of all things, and in him all things live and move and have their being (Acts 17:28).

The materialist says, "Yes, I understand there has to be something that is self-existent and eternal, that must have the power of being within itself. I don't want to retreat—as many of my colleagues do—to an idea of self-creation; I grant that that's absurd. We must have a self-existent, eternal something. But I'm not going to grant to you, my Christian friend, that this self-existent, eternal something is God—that he is a transcendent being. Rather, he is either *part* of the universe or the *sum total of the universe*."

But if we're going to say that the eternal something is the sum total of the universe, then we have to include the piece of chalk. Yet we know that my piece of chalk is not self-existent and eternal, because this piece of chalk can disintegrate. I can break it in half. I can reduce it; I can change it. It goes through process.

"Well," the materialist says, "the chalk's individuated, particular existence, right now, is contingent and all that; but underlying it somehow is some universal or elemental pulsating force that is the cause of the existence of everything that is. And it is this yet undiscovered core or pulsating center of the universe that is self-existent and eternal. This is the part that accounts for the explosion of that point of singularity, and all of the power of being is compacted and compressed into this little point. Then everything else, ultimately, is generated through the power that comes from this pulsating source."

The word *generated* will of course call to mind the first book of the Old Testament, Genesis. Its name comes from the Greek word that means to be, to become, or to happen. To make something come into existence is to generate it, to cause it to be. So here, according to the materialist, we have this isolated, hidden, unknown point within the universe that is the pulsating core of all reality that generates everything from the beginning. The materialist view is that there is no God who lives outside the universe, who is above and beyond the universe, but that this self-existent, eternal generating power is part of the universe itself.

This immanentistic view that is very popular in certain circles in science and philosophy today is of a self-existent, eternal power, without which there can be nothing. But why do we Christians say that it has to be *outside* of the universe? That is the challenge they raise to us. Why do we say it has to transcend the universe; why can't it be a part of the universe itself? My answer is, it *can* be a part of the universe itself, depending on how we define universe. If you mean by "universe" "all that is," and if God *is,* then God would be subsumed under the term *universe* because it describes all that is. But if you mean by "universe" the created universe, then obviously we cannot subsume God into the meaning of the term *universe.*

Christians say that God *transcends* the universe. But transcendence is not a description of God's location. Transcendence is not a geographical description. We are not saying that God is transcendent in the sense that he lives somewhere out there, east of the sun and west of the moon. What is meant by transcendence, in philosophy and theology, is a *higher order of being.* That is, rather than transcendence being a geographical description, it is an *ontological* description. When we say that God is transcendent we mean, simply, that he is a higher order of being than we are. He is a higher order of being than my chalk. He is a higher order of being than the sun. He is a higher order of being than pure energy. That is what we mean by transcendence: God is a higher order of being.

If the materialist retreats to some unknown, invisible, immeasurable, pulsating point or core within the boundaries of the universe that is self-existent and eternal, from which everything else is generated, ultimately he is saying that there is something that transcends everything else in the universe—something that transcends all those things that are dependent, derived, and contingent. Now we are just arguing over its name, over whether the name of this transcendent thing is 'X' or Yahweh. No matter how we slice it, we are forced back to a self-existent, eternal being from whose being and from whose power all things come into existence.

Many Christians object at this point, "Okay, we grant that philosophy and reason argue and demonstrate that you have to have a self-existent, eternal something. But how do we get from that to the God of the Bible? So far, all we have is Aristotle's 'unmoved mover'; all we have so far is an abstract idea of a self-existent, eternal being. You haven't come yet to the God of the Bible. What is the connection," they ask, "between the God of the Bible and the god of the philosophers?" Most of what I have been saying in the last several chapters about the question of the existence of God has been based more on philosophy than on biblical exegesis. In our next chapter we will consider the relationship between the god of the philosophers and the God of the Bible.

SECTION V
God and the Philosophers

16

THE GOD OF THE PHILOSOPHERS
AND THE GOD OF THE BIBLE

In our argument for the existence of God we have focused on the concept of *necessary being,* or an eternal, self-existent being. These terms are abstract and lack the warmth of the biblical view of God. He is a God who has a personal name and a God who is profoundly involved in creation. But his care of the world does not end with its mere creation. Rather it extends to his providential sustaining of the world and his governance over that world. Most importantly, he is a God who works to redeem the world that is fallen. This God of the Bible cannot be identified with the God of the philosophers. He may have certain similarities to the philosophers' deity but he cannot be reduced to a mere impersonal force or abstract philosophical principle.

In ancient philosophy, the concept of God was a necessary philosophical principle to give unity to the diversity of the external world. "God" was an intellectual concept of "ultimate reality" that varied from Thales' concept of physical monism to the pre-Socratic notion of "mind" (*Nous*) or Logic (*Logos*) to give order and harmony to reality. Add to these notions Plato's idea of the "Good" and Aristotle's "Unmoved Mover," and we begin to grasp the focus on an impersonal force or forces that served as deities.

Aristotle spoke of God in various ways. In addition to the idea of Unmoved Mover, or First Cause, he described God as

"Pure Form" and as "Thought Thinking Itself" or even as "Pure Actuality."

We could also say of *the God of the Bible* that he is the first cause, he is the divine Logos, he is pure form and ultimate mind. These things could be truly said of him. He is *at least* necessary being. He is *at least* an eternal, self-existent being. We understand that God is *more* than these things, but by no means is he *less* than these things.

God Is Not Just the Unmoved Mover

The God revealed in Scripture, indeed, in its very first verses, is much more than the "Unmoved Mover," who "creates" out of philosophical necessity. In the Creation account, we are introduced to a God who acts *voluntarily* and *decisively,* bringing order and fullness by his creative word. Creation reveals his immeasurable power, eternality, and transcendence. His acts are reasonable and full of purpose. The entire cosmos is sustained by his grace and shows his commitment to his people (originally the Israelites) and to the covenant he established with them. The whole story of *redemption* portrayed in Scripture begins in *Creation.* God is a God who lovingly created and upholds his creation, and who is intimately concerned with the affairs of history.

Christians often object to God's being compared *at all* to abstract philosophical views. The God of the Bible has so little in common with the gods of philosophy that some think *any* comparison is out of order. If Christians reject my approach for this reason, then I must remind them of one simple fact about God as he is revealed in Scripture: he is incomprehensible. That does not mean he is completely unknowable; rather, it simply means that we can never have a complete or exhaustive knowledge of who God is.

That our knowledge of God is *partial,* however, does not indicate that it is either *invaluable* or *untrue.* If we were required to have a comprehensive or total understanding of the nature of God before we could be assured that we had a true knowledge of him, we would have to reject Christian theism altogether. Christian theology asserts the incomprehensibility of God, a notion that is not only biblical but philosophical as well. As John Calvin expressed it, the finite cannot grasp the infinite (*finitum non capax infiniti*). No creature, being finite, no matter the level of its intelligence or scope of its knowledge, could possibly fathom entirely the depth of an infinite being. To have an exhaustive or comprehensive understanding of an infinite being, one would have to be infinite. Even in heaven, though the Christian will have far more understanding than presently enjoyed, that understanding will not reach the level of the infinite.

If *partial* knowledge is by its very "partialness" untrue or inadequate, then we would be forced to say that not only our reflections on natural theology are invalid but all that we learn from the Bible would also be untrue and inadequate.

Thomas Aquinas wrestled with this difficulty of the partial character of natural theology. He said of our natural knowledge of God that it is *mediated, analogous,* and *incomplete,* but *true.*

What we have endeavored to prove by rational arguments is the same thing that Aristotle and other pagan philosophers have demonstrated: the ultimate cause of the universe is *uncaused, eternal,* and lacking in nothing whatsoever. We have shown that one of the most important attributes of the first cause of the universe (aseity, or self-existence) coincides neatly with the God of the Bible. If that is all we have achieved in our apologetic, then we rejoice that we have defended Christian theism at its most critical point of attack. The simple fact that portions of Aristotle's thought can coincide with Christian doctrine does not vitiate the biblical record. In fact, it bolsters the Bible's claim.

We agree with Aristotle that the universe has to have a first cause, and that that first cause has to be self-existent. We agree that the first cause's metaphysical grandeur can be neither improved upon nor depreciated. But we also assert—contrary to Aristotle— that that first cause is *immanent* in and with his creation, and therefore providentially governs events *in time*. Christians do not have to negotiate the truth of God's Word at this point, for both the Bible and God's revelation of himself in nature complementarily affirm this truth.

We also assert God's *transcendence*. It is that attribute that is constantly under attack from both within and without the church. The one thing that stands out among the various non-Christian philosophers (e.g., deists, pantheists, atheists) throughout the centuries is their insistence on undermining the transcendental aspect of God's sovereignty (and, as a result, his immanence, as well). Whether they affirm the existence of the divine or not, the end result is the same: escape from the subservience demanded by an omnipotent Creator. For the deist, God is so far removed that he can command nothing of his creation; for the pantheist, God is part and parcel of the created world and is therefore equally powerless to exercise dominion; as for the atheist, God's existence is simply denied. For all three positions, the point is the same: there is no one greater than ourselves who will hold us accountable for our actions.

God Is the Intentional Designer

Despite our positive gain in establishing the crucial biblical doctrine of God's self-existence, we still need to bridge the gap between the self-existent, eternal something and a personal God. One of the famous arguments for God's existence, which we mentioned earlier, is the *teleological* argument, the argument from design in the universe to a Creator God. The actual word *telos* is from the Greek and means "end, purpose, or goal." The teleological argument for God starts from the notion that the world of experience, that is, the world we experience, has an observable purpose to it and must therefore be the result of an ultimate designer. Even the two greatest skeptics in modern history—Kant and Hume—saw the teleological argument as the preeminent argument for God's existence. Kant himself mentions in passing that the two things he could never ignore in this world are the starry skies above and the moral law within. Kant was more than a philosopher; he was a scientist as well. He was overwhelmed by the evidentiary presence of design in the world of nature. This much is obvious for us: one cannot attribute design to nature without begging the question of a designer. One necessarily follows from the other. But this is where the debate centered: can there be such a thing as unintentional design? Can the world *look* designed but in reality be a random sample of space plus time plus chance?

The main problem we face here is that the theist and atheist will seldom agree on what constitutes "design." English philosopher Antony Flew's (1919–) parable about a garden might help us better understand this point:[1]

> Two explorers came upon a clearing in the jungle. In the clearing were growing many flowers and many weeds. One explorer says, "Some gardener must tend this plot." The other disagrees, "There is no gardener." So they pitch their tents and set a watch. No gardener is ever seen. "But perhaps he is an invisible gardener." So they set up a barbed-wire fence. They electrify it. They patrol with bloodhounds. (For they remember how H. G. Wells's *The Invisible Man* could be both smelt and touched though he could not be seen.) But no shrieks ever suggest that some intruder has received a shock. No movements of the wire ever betray an invisible climber. The bloodhounds never give cry. Yet still the believer is not convinced. "But there is a gardener, invisible, intangible, insensible to electric shocks, a gardener who has no scent and makes no sound, a gardener who comes secretly to look after the garden he loves." At last the Sceptic despairs. "But what remains of the original assertion? Just how does what you call an invisible, intangible, eternally elusive gardener differ from an imaginary gardener or even from no gardener at all?"[1]

In this parable, Flew suggests that meaningful talk about God is impossible. While we have already discussed the logical inconsistencies of such a position, it is important to point out that we have not been engaged in this type of discourse at all. Rather, we have been discussing rational proofs that carry the weight of logical compulsion, which in turn serve as a most compelling evidence for God's existence. In other words, we have been discussing the all-important question about what needs to exist if the universe is dependent. The simple answer is, if the universe is dependent then there has to be an independent God. Secondly, we will discuss (chapters 20-23) the biblical record and its basic reliability. We will see that we are dealing with concrete historical events, not imaginary ones. Finally, this supposedly "invisible, intangible [and] eternally elusive gardener" has quite unexpectedly come in the flesh. Nobody since then has been able to falsify this claim. And this is largely our point: belief in God is open to verification. Whether Flew wants to admit it or not, Christianity claims far more than wishful thinking. We are not merely discussing our feelings, as Flew would have us believe, even though our emotions do indeed play a part in our apologetic (as is also true of the unbeliever—see chapter 19). That is, the believer sees a tended garden while the skeptic sees a discombobulated mass of organic growth. But the obvious answer to Flew's question, "how does what you call an invisible, intangible, eternally elusive gardener differ from an imaginary gardener or even from no gardener at all?" is simply that the skeptic has still not accounted for the garden itself. In other words, the burden of proof lies on the skeptic who desires to do away with the obvious order of the universe, substituting for it random chance. Just a "smidgen" of design is all it takes to have a designer.

In fact, the observable design present in the world is exactly what enabled the closet atheists of the Enlightenment to become deists. Hiding out in the church, these nonbelievers found in deism a philosophy they could live with: they disbelieved the essentials of the Christian faith but could not avoid the implications of design. So they posited the existence of a Creator who created the world much like a perfectly constructed clock. Who would deny that a watchmaker existed if they came across a watch in the sand on a beach? *Design necessarily includes intention.* But intention does not just exist, floating around in space, creating and exhibiting design. No, intention is always attached to intelligence. Indeed, the single most important characteristic of personality is intention. For intention to exist, something must be acting with purpose. One cannot have design accidentally. Design requires purpose, and purpose requires intention. We cannot have intention unintentionally. Blind force cannot be involved in intelligent selection.

Self-existent, formless, eternal *matter* has no personality. Impersonal forces have no mind, no will, and therefore cannot design anything. We recognize that personal reality exists in the universe. Descartes' argument for his own existence was a proof of his own personhood—a personhood that contained thought and intention, the ingredients of personality, within it.

God Is Personal and He Holds Us Accountable

It is a short step from the reality of a self-existent eternal being to a self-existent eternal personal being who designs the universe by his own mind and will.

But it is precisely because God is personal and has a mind and will that his very existence is attacked. If God were conceived of as an amorphous, undefined "higher power" or impersonal force, there would be little theological fuss about him. No one fears judgment at the hands of cosmic dust. Who is called to repent before an impersonal force? The ungodly seek an impersonal and ignorant God precisely because we are personal beings and we know we are ultimately accountable to our Creator for our behavior.

This aspect of personal accountability drove Kant to consider theism from a different direction. He moved his focus from the theoretical to the practical in his considerations and (as we will see in chapter 17) argued *for* the existence of God on ethical grounds.

Without a God who is at once transcendent and immanent, there is no judgment and no accountability. Once this is denied,

concepts like "accidental purpose" become imaginable. It becomes
believable that the world portrays design even though a personal
designer does not exist; but all we are left with at this point is
unintentional intention, which is as absurd as the idea of self-creation. If, however, we come to the conclusion that there is design
in the universe, we know from our apologetic that there must be a
self-existent, eternal something that is responsible for generating
the universe; and that self-existent, eternal something must also
have intention; and if intention, it must also be personal; and if
personal, then we have moved away from any abstractions proffered by the Greek philosophers and have landed squarely on the
testimony of the sacred Scriptures.

17

KANT'S MORAL ARGUMENT

We have already explored Immanuel Kant's epistemological revolution. We will now turn to the argument for God's existence that he thought was most plausible: the moral argument. Even though Kant was a theist, his philosophy had led him to a type of theological agnosticism. He believed that theoretical discussions about God are really exercises in futility because our experiences here in the phenomenal world can never lead us to a fruitful knowledge of the Creator, who is in the unreachable noumenal world. While Kant believed in God, he insisted that God could not be proven to exist by using theoretical arguments. As we mentioned earlier, he argued that all of the traditional proofs for God's existence were invalid. But he still desired to leave room for faith in the lives of intelligent people. Though the "starry skies above" were not enough for Kant to conclude the existence of God, the "moral law within" *was* enough.

In his *Critique of Practical Reason*, Kant approached the question of God's existence through practical considerations. He asked, What would have to be the case in order for morality to be meaningful? In his *Critique of Pure Reason*, Kant had impolitely ushered God out the front door by undermining the traditional proofs; but in his *Critique of Practical Reason*, Kant ran around to the kitchen and let God in again through the back door. He did this through his moral argument. Before we attempt to expound on it, we shall first look at what the Scriptures say regarding morality and the existence of God.

Romans 1: God's Moral Law Is Plain to All

In Romans 1, Paul charges that, because God's eternal power and divine nature are clearly perceived in the things he has made, all people are without excuse when it comes to acknowledging the Creator God. Then, starting at verse 28, Paul goes on to the subject of morality:

> And since they did not see fit to acknowledge God, God gave them up to a debased mind to do what ought not to be done. They were filled with all manner of unrighteousness, evil, covetousness, malice. They are full of envy, murder, strife, deceit, maliciousness. They are gossips, slanderers, haters of God, insolent, haughty, boastful, inventors of evil, disobedient to parents, foolish, faithless, heartless, ruthless (vv. 28-31).

While this list is not exhaustive, it does catalog some of the main ways humans violate each other through immoral behavior. Sin, unbridled, carries with it a hatred for absolute moral values.

The crux of the matter comes, however, in verse 32:

> Though they know God's decree that those who practice such things deserve to die, they not only do them but give approval to those who practice them.

Who are "they" that "know God's decree"? They are the very people who practice the sins previously listed. It is as if Paul is saying, "Given that God has clearly revealed himself (including his holy character) in the things he has made, we humans know of God's righteousness and what that demands of our behavior." In other words, every one of us knows the difference between right and wrong. We know how we *ought* to act, Paul argues (vv. 28, 32), because the absolute, infinite, and almighty God is holy. People know they *ought* not do each of the sins Paul names. Regardless of having this sense of oughtness, however, we not only chase after such sins and approve of them in others, we actually enlist the support of other people and encourage them to participate in the same devious acts. This is the essence of sin: direct rebellion in the face of the living God. Having refused to acknowledge God's goodness to us (Rom. 1:21, 28), we ignore what we *ought* to do and focus exclusively on what we *want* to do.

Further on in Romans, Paul's indictment against humanity becomes clearly inescapable. In 2:12, 14, he writes,

> For all who have sinned without the law will also perish with-out the law, and all who have sinned under the law will be judged by the law. . . . For when Gentiles, who do not have the law, by nature do what the law requires, they are a law to themselves, even though they do not have the law.

The law, in this text, quite obviously stands in judgment on the individual. In fact, it stands in judgment upon those to whom it was not even given (i.e., the Gentiles). Not only did God give his chosen people the Law (this includes the entire Old Testament), he actually has written his law upon the hearts of every human being. The perfect ethic revealed in the law of God delivered to Moses and the Prophets after him, is the same perfect ethic revealed in the law God gives internally to all people. Therefore, a defense based on ignorance of the law revealed to the Israelites is entirely irrelevant. One crucial point Paul makes is that the measure of revelation given to a person is not the issue; rather, the response on the part of that person is the issue (whatever the degree of revelation) and will be what God takes into account on the final day. All people, then, both Jew and Gentile, stand judged by the holy law of God, which law he has revealed both in the outward things created by him and in the inward things written on the hearts of every human. No one can escape the moral law of a righteous God.

Non-Christians often assert that our consciences are simply a result of societal taboos or cultural conventions. Yet even though we may debate what belongs to custom and what belongs to absolute law, we cannot eradicate the conscience. No culture is devoid of an ethical structure, because if it were, it would cease to be a viable culture. Social interaction would be all but impossible in a society that has no ability to determine right from wrong. As much as naïve utopianism desires it, if man had no God, and subsequently no morality from which he could borrow, the last thing there would be is peace.

Our relativistic culture today attempts to get around the need for a moral law by declaring that there is no right or wrong at all, that every act is *amoral* (neither moral nor immoral). This is nothing more than an educated barbarism; and despite its efforts to the contrary, the conscience cannot be eradicated.

Kant's "Categorical Imperative"

Kant's moral argument comes in precisely at this point. In the *Critique of Practical Reason,* he argues that every single person in the world has a sense of "oughtness," an inherent sense of right and wrong. This sense Kant calls the "categorical imperative." It cannot be ignored, and it drives every person to behave in a certain manner. It is "categorical" because it is universal: everybody has a category of understanding regarding morality. It is "imperative" because this moral category impels the person to act upon it; it represents an absolute command. This is by no means moral relativism. Kant contends that, since all people desire to be happy, the only way to that happiness is through the moral life (i.e., the categorical imperative). All people share an objective sense of duty which obligates them to act accordingly. Whenever we try to erase it, deny it, or flee from it, only guilt follows, while the categorical imperative still remains.

Guilt is the one thing that always redirects the conversation between the apologist and his or her listener. Guilt is the one thing that most people seem to have and yet it is the one thing that most people have not yet resolved. Ignoring this categorical imperative will not make it go away; in fact, it only produces more feelings of guilt. Kant argues that such feelings of guilt come from failing to do our duty, from failing to follow the categorical imperative, or those things we are morally obligated to do.

Kant used a transcendental approach to the question. Given that we all have the categorical imperative, what conditions would have to exist for this imperative to be meaningful? Given that guilt exists from our failure to fulfill our duties, what must be the case in order for there to be this awareness of moral absolutes? He did not attempt to show empirically how our knowledge of moral obligations takes place, nor did he begin his task by supposing that such knowledge was even possible; rather, he sought to rise above that problem and approach it by asking, *If* such knowledge is possible, what would have to be? While the nihilists would later argue that that sense of "oughtness" is just a glitch in the human composition, and that it is meaningless and must therefore be shrugged off, Kant sought to find out what would be necessary for true ethics—an ethic that imposes obligations—to be meaningful. Practically speaking, Kant understood that without some objective standard of behavior, civilizations would falter and fall. The law of the land would be simply "might makes right," and all people would be reduced to nameless, faceless stepping stones for the one with the largest gun. To a certain degree, such is the precarious position we find ourselves in today.

If there were no God, then there would be no ultimate ground for doing what is right. All things would be permissible, because all choices would reduce to a battle over *preferences*. Every person would do what is right in his or her own mind, which would create conflict and warfare between classes, races, and individuals. Without rules that rest on solid foundations, our own individual "rights" would take precedence over everyone else's.

Kant: Morality Makes No Sense Without God

Kant was acutely aware that the stability of society was at stake, so he attempted to answer his transcendental question, "What would it take for objective moral standards to be meaningful?" with a series of solutions. The first thing that is necessary for ethics to be meaningful, said Kant, is *justice*. If crime ultimately pays, then there is no practical reason to be virtuous. Practically, we have no reason to be anything but selfish. For moral standards to be meaningful, right behavior must be rewarded and wrong behavior must be punished.

But after this has been established, what would be necessary for justice to take place? Since justice obviously is not dispensed perfectly in this life, Kant said, it must be doled out perfectly in a state beyond this life. Because in this life "innocent" people perish at the hands of the wicked, there must be life after death, or a place where the wicked will get their just deserts. Consider how the saint long ago puzzled over the same question: "O LORD, how long shall the wicked, how long shall the wicked exult?" (Ps. 94:3; cf. Pss. 37; 73). The wicked can exult only in a place where justice is not perfectly carried out. There is no absolute justice in this world. Nonetheless we seek justice, and we have courts to dispense justice, even though justice is not always served. There must be, then, according to Kant, perfect justice somewhere, and that somewhere is in the life hereafter.

Kant saw the possibility, however, that even if there is life after death, we may still carry with us the same faults as before, and so perfect justice would remain elusive. Another thing required for perfect justice to be dispensed after this life is a *morally perfect judge*. If this judge suffered any moral weakness, then ultimately that judge would not be righteous. He could make the same mistakes we make here on earth in our courtrooms.

Thus far, we see in Kant's argument that in order to have ethical standards, there must be perfect justice; and in order to have perfect justice, a perfect judge must exist—one who is above reproach and beyond corruption. But what must this judge have in order to be morally perfect and make perfect judgments? The answer Kant offered was "omniscience." Suppose this morally perfect judge did the best job possible according to his character, but unfortunately he was limited in his knowledge so that he was liable to make mistakes. Only an all-knowing judge could know all the facts or extenuating circumstances in the cases that come before his bench. This perfect judge cannot be subject to the "accidents" that result from ignorance. The judge must know all of the facts, so that the judgment rendered is without error or blemish.

But would the presence of a morally perfect and omniscient judge ensure perfect justice? Not yet. The judgment passed might fail to be carried out—unless that judge has the perfect power or ability to carry out every judgment that proceeds from his mouth. *Omnipotence,* then, is the final factor needed in this judge. He must be perfectly able to enforce his judgments in order to guarantee that perfect justice would take place. So this judge, finally, must be omnipotent, stronger than any counter-force that could possibly hinder his judgments from being carried out. To summarize, in order for ethical standards to have any absolute meaning (thereby imposing obligations upon us), justice must exist; and, granted that our justice is imperfect on earth, there must be perfect justice in the hereafter; and that perfect justice must be secured by a morally perfect, omniscient, and omnipotent judge.

Kant is arguing transcendentally. Rather than giving us empirical evidence that moral absolutes exist, he has given us what is necessary in order for there to be moral absolutes. If our sense of "oughtness" is going to matter, then that means that our lives matter. If this much is true, then it follows that life will continue after death, because these moral absolutes were given by an absolute being—which being will hold us accountable for every single act ever done or left undone in this life. This judge is in no way comparable to our earthly judges, for this one knows all and is all-powerful; and what is more, he is entirely holy and utterly committed to righteousness. He cannot be bribed, nor can he be persuaded to overlook any guilt. Morality, Kant argued, if taken truly and seriously, makes the affirmation of God a practical necessity. We must live as if there is indeed a God, because if there is not, then we have no hope for civilization and for human community.

18

THE NIHILISTS

Those philosophers who came after Kant, most notably Friedrich Nietzsche (1844–1900), understood Kant's point: that nearly all of those who do not affirm the existence of God nonetheless try to live according to some ethical standard and so are actually living on borrowed capital (that of the theists). Kant's heirs—the nihilists—rightly saw this fault in the "man on the street," and they argued, as did Kant, that we cannot have both. We either have God and meaningful morality and meaningful lives, or we have no God, and all of life is meaningless, without any trace of hope.

Nietzsche and the "New Morality" of Nihilism

Nietzsche, one of the most important thinkers after Kant, recognized that every civilization in the West since the first century had been built upon a Judeo-Christian foundation. And he saw Western civilization as decadent precisely *because* it was built on Judeo-Christian principles. These principles, in Nietzsche's eyes, undermined the very essence of human existence. Man's basic trait, said Nietzsche, is found in his will-to-power. The Judeo-Christian ethic suppresses that will-to-power and elevates a "herd morality" that exalts attributes of human weakness such as compassion. Indeed God himself is dead, said Nietzsche, having perished by a terminal case of pity. It is not enough to live "as if" God exists, said Nietzsche. That's like Alice in Wonderland. The fact that the alternatives to theism are grim (no justice, no absolutes, etc.) is no reason to assume the existence of God. Kant's morality, being a generic "Christian" morality, would only get in the way of those who desire to rise above the meaninglessness of life and become their own masters. As Nietzsche fully understood, once God is seen to be dead, natural rights, morality, and the idea of progress become total shams. All the old values held with such fervor in the history of Western culture will lose their vitality and validity. Facing this prospect of pure nihilism, Nietzsche called for a "new morality," a morality carved out by a "Superman" who would rise above the morality of the herd. This Superman would have the courage to create his own morality. Yet all the time he exercised his courage he would know that, in the end, even this courage was doomed to meaninglessness.

The greatest contribution of the nihilists is their pointing out the clear-cut consequences of what life would be without the existence of God. They reject half-hearted, compromise positions that hesitate to embrace either full-orbed theism or total nihilism.

Ecclesiastes on Nihilism

The history of philosophy and theoretical thought lies on a continuum. At one end we have full-bodied theism (or historic, orthodox Trinitarianism); and at the other end is nihilism. Nihilism argues that there is no God, and from that premise nihilism concludes that there is no meaning, significance, or sense to human existence.

This tension between theism and nihilism is not new. It was an issue in antiquity, as seen in the wisdom literature of the Old Testament. These two opposing worldviews are juxtaposed clearly in the book of Ecclesiastes.

This fascinating book explores the implications of secularism and offers a positive assessment of faith in the living God. It compares having faith in a mercifully giving God with the grim alternative, life as utter uselessness. During a literal debate with himself, the Preacher of Ecclesiastes intends to show how his experiences "under the sun," that is, apart from faith, lead to the idea, shared by the later nihilists and existentialists, that life is absurd. He does this in order to motivate the reader to draw the proper conclusion that life without God is completely futile (i.e., we must "fear God," Eccles. 12:13). Translating this into Kantian terms, the Preacher of Ecclesiastes sets out to "know wisdom and to know madness and folly" (1:17), or the profit of human activity within the phenomenal world, the world as it appears to us. Through empirical observation, the Preacher attempts to find meaning in his experiences. He attempts to make sense of this life by focusing on everything "under the sun." What were his findings in the end? "The wise person has his eyes in his head, but the fool walks in darkness. And yet I perceived that the same event happens to all of them. . . . How the wise dies just like the fool! So I hated life, because what is done under the sun was grievous to me, for all is vanity and a striving after wind" (2:14, 16b-17). From the perspective of the skeptic, the one who disbelieves the existence of an all-sustaining being in whom the very grounds of meaning consist, every human activity is utterly useless and subject to chaos. The very condition of humanity is insubstantial, a chasing after the wind.

The existentialist playwright, novelist, and philosopher Jean-Paul Sartre (1905–1980) defined man as a "useless passion."[1] Describing the human condition in his book *Nausea,* Sartre defined man as a being made up primarily of passions. As Sartre rightly perceived, all of those passions are completely worthless and meaningless, all of our cares come to nothing, if there is no God.

By drawing on his empirical observations (from the phenomenal world), the author of Ecclesiastes concludes that life is a vicious cycle; it is completely devoid of purpose. But he does not stop there. Instead of buying into Kant's radical disjunction between the world of nature and the world of grace (or the "phenomenal" and "noumenal" worlds), the Preacher goes beyond his empirical observations and begins to make assertions about things *above* the sun, about the metaphysical realm. He calls for faith in the Creator: "Remember also your Creator in the days of your youth, before the evil days come . . . and the spirit returns to God who gave it" (12:1a, 7b). The Preacher looks past the sun itself. Nihilism restrains the sight of the nihilists to this world alone, and hope dies along with the very meaning of their lives. Ecclesiastes calls us to place our faith in God's great wisdom (8:17); in God's exhaustive goodness (8:15); in God's perfect justice (8:11-13); and finally, in God's holy wrath to punish hypocrisy (5:1-6). As many theologians have concluded regarding the message of Ecclesiastes, the Preacher addresses those whose view is bound by the finitude of this world; he explores life from their perspective, and attempts to show them how it is inherently useless. Ecclesiastes is, in the end, a scathing critique against nihilism and those who, as we mentioned above, desire to hold on to the moral framework of Christianity while at the same time denying God's existence.

Secular Humanism: Combining Theism and Nihilism

Rarely do philosophers embrace pure nihilism, opting instead for an intermediate position. But as they seek to find positions somewhere between theism and nihilism, they always borrow capital from one or the other pole. One case in point would be the modern-day "secular humanist." The secular humanist somewhat naïvely wants us to deny the existence of God, presume our beginnings to be a result of chaotic chance (rendering both our origin and our destiny meaningless), and yet still calls us to fight for human rights and dignity. If ever there was a "striving after the wind" (see Eccles. 1:14, 17), this is it. Secular humanism rests on pure sentimentality; it merely feels good to protect human rights and dignity. But such persons are intellectual cowards. They don't have the stomach to go where their atheism drives them: full-fledged nihilism. Instead, they choose to blissfully live on borrowed capital. Why does human dignity matter if we are all cosmic accidents? The very source of human dignity comes from the dignity of the Creator, from our having been created in his image. Indeed, the secular humanist is in a compromised position. Remember, Kant saw the threat of nihilism coming as more people began rejecting the traditional arguments for God, so he posited his moral argument in an attempt to curb the consequence of denying God's existence (i.e., nihilism). Nietzsche also saw this. But more importantly for us, so did Paul. For "you were at that time separated from Christ, . . . and strangers to the covenants of promise, *having no hope* and without God in the world" (Eph. 2:12, emphasis added). Even more poignant is the apostle's letter to the Corinthian church: "And if Christ has not been raised, your faith is futile and you are still in your sins. Then those also who have fallen asleep in Christ have perished. If in this life only we have hoped in Christ, we are of all people most to be pitied" (1 Cor. 15:17-19). Paul is saying that if Jesus has remained in the grave, then do not be mad at the Christian believer, rather pity him. Paul and the others with him are to be pitied because they have wasted their lives by devoting themselves to the legacy of a dead man. There is a one-to-one correlation between having hope and having faith in the God of the universe. If one denies God, then one has no basis for hope whatsoever. The only alternative is hopelessness.

The nihilists who came after Kant saw this, and their desire was to be consistent. If we cannot know God exists, they argued, wishful thinking (which is exactly how they viewed Kant's moral argument) is not enough. We must face up to the utter uselessness of life. It is grim, yes, but we must have the courage to live life anyway, and we must avoid the escapism of religion at all costs. Karl Marx called religion the opiate of the masses. Sigmund Freud called it a crutch. Religion, to these men, was nothing more than the ultimate escape from the reality of nihilism—that everything is absurd. Religion, to them, was the most effective drug to dull the senses and minimize the pain of meaninglessness. Religious people, according to this view, are nothing more than hedonists whose pleasure is found in escaping the futile passions, labor, and ultimately, death, that make up this useless life.

If There Is No God, Why Is There Religion?

Atheists such as these did not waste their time on disproving the existence of God. Kant had already shattered the traditional arguments for God. By relegating God to the sphere of the unknowable, Kant had effectively opened the door for nihilists to assume that, since God is entirely beyond understanding, his existence is irrelevant. The question atheists like Freud attempted to answer was not, "Is there a God?" but, "Why are human being so incurably religious?"

Freud and others could not deny that religious belief is virtually universal. Indeed religion is so prevalent on the planet that we can say of man that he is not only *homo sapiens*; he is also *homo religiosus*.

Atheists understand that the presence of religion does not prove the existence of God. But it nettles them that so many people are religious. They seek, then, to give a rational explanation for the phenomena of religion. The question is not, "Is there a God?" The question becomes, "Since there is no God, why is there religion?"

Though many answers have been given to this question, the most frequent answer is psychological fear. Mortals, according to this view, simply cannot bear to live in a universe where nobody is at home in heaven. They cannot face life in an indifferent universe where there is no ultimate cure for our troubles. Since we cannot bear the grim alternative to a universe without a Creator, we run into the arms of religion, declare that God exists, and leave it at that. It is virtual thumb-sucking religiosity. This was the accepted argument against theism well into the twentieth century. But one must wonder, at least from a Christian perspective, whether the psychological need, or crutch, may in fact be for the leg of the atheist, and not for the theist.

19

THE PSYCHOLOGY OF ATHEISM

As we have seen, atheists often dismiss the Christian's belief in God as a direct result of psychological need. "If God does not exist," they ask, "why are people so religious?" We desire to pose the same question back to them: If there is a God, why are there atheists? And our answer is similar to theirs, except that the Scriptures offer a far more persuasive case than, for example, the embarrassing psychoanalysis of Sigmund Freud. In *Civilization and Its Discontents,* Freud wrote that religious needs derive from "the infant's helplessness and the longing for the father" and that this vulnerability is permanently sustained by "fear of the superior power of Fate."[1] Quite to the contrary, we believe that those like Freud who reject God do so in order to escape the helplessness that one feels in the face of the holy and "superior power" of the God who really exists.

One of the most difficult problems we face as we look at the history of philosophy is that brilliant thinkers have landed on opposite ends of the pole. On one end we see the likes of John Stuart Mill and Friedrich Nietzsche, and on the other, Aurelius Augustine and Thomas Aquinas. While it is obvious to church people which philosophers are "greater," we cannot deny that many exceptional minds have come to the conclusion that there is no God. It is not simply a situation of Christian thinkers having superior intellects. Rather, we must agree with our atheist counterparts that the question of the existence of God is indeed freighted with psychological baggage. We also agree that people are capable of looking at the evidence through a lens that favors their own biases.

As Christians, every fiber of our being wants God to exist, and every fiber of our being is equally repulsed by the thought that the sum total of our lives is Sartre's "useless passion." And we must admit that it is quite plausible for us to construct philosophical and theological systems on the basis of our own desires and prejudices, which serve to cloud our thinking. But Christians are not the only targets of this criticism. Atheists can be charged with the same sort of intellectual prejudice.

Both sides of the debate must see that everybody who gets involved in a discussion about the existence of God brings psychological baggage to the table. Those who deny God, for example, have an enormous vested interest in their denial because, simply put, if the biblical God exists, then an infinite obstacle stands between them and their own autonomy. Man cannot be the ultimate creator of his own destiny if the sovereign God of the universe exists. Freud knew this in his own way. For him, the Christians had to be the weak ones, the ones whose faith he reduced to infantile helplessness. Ironically for Freud, however, the Scriptures describe the psychology of atheists in much the same way as Freud describes theists. Nothing stands more firmly in the way of our own autonomous desires than a self-existent, eternally righteous and just God. There is, by Freud's own admission, a universal knowledge that the worst thing imaginable would be to fall into the hands of "the superior power of fate." This fear is infinitely aggravated, however, when that "fate" is viewed as a holy God. Just as we are capable of inventing gods where there are none, so we are capable of doing everything possible to deny our guilt before a God who actually exists.

There is as much psychological pressure for the atheist to deny the existence of God as there is for the theist to embrace his existence. According to the Bible, fallen man will not entertain thoughts of the divine. Our natural moral condition includes with it a reprobate mind, that is, a mind so darkened by prejudice that we do not want to even open the window a crack to allow the rays of God's self-revelation into our heads. We know what is at stake if we do this; we know that we are in trouble if we acknowledge the existence of a sovereign God.

We have looked at the first chapter of Romans several times already. We have seen that one of the greatest conflicts we have with theologians and philosophers in the Kantian camp is that they deny that God can be known through nature. He *can* be known—not in a saving way, to be sure—but known in such a way that we are left, according to the apostle Paul, "without excuse" (cf. Rom. 1:19-20). What becomes clear in Paul's argument in this first chapter is that the main problem with those who deny the existence of God is *not* intellectual. It is not because of insufficient information, or that God's manifestation of himself in nature has been obscured. The atheists' problem is not that they cannot know God, rather it is they do not *want* to know him. For Paul, man's problem with the existence of God is not an intellectual problem; it is a *moral* problem. "For the wrath of God is revealed from heaven against all ungodliness and unrighteousness of men . . ." (Rom. 1:18). Strikingly, the God of the apostle reveals his wrath. This makes God even more repulsive to the atheist. Even many theists, unfortunately, refuse to acknowledge that the Scriptures reveal that God is a God of wrath. But Paul does not mince his words: the God of the universe is furious at those "who by their unrighteousness suppress the truth" (Rom. 1:18b). God's anger boils over when those he has created in his image intentionally stifle the clear revelation of God in nature. The apostle's radical declaration is that every human being who has ever lived knows that God exists because God has shown himself in the created order. His wrath is kindled against those who hold that clear manifestation down.

In modern psychological categories, we might translate

Paul's discussion in the following terms: What thoughts are we
likely to suppress? Happy thoughts, or traumatic experiences? It
is most likely the latter. The psychologist is well aware that, even
though these thoughts are suppressed, they still exist; that is,
the most traumatic experiences are often buried deepest within
our consciences. Such repressed memories come out in various ways. The psychologist probes the mind through inkblots,
symbolic associations, dreams, and so forth. The psychologist
attempts to discover what the patient is suppressing and to what
extent. We are masters at suppression. Paul's chosen word for
suppression (in Greek, *katechein*) suggests the act of pushing or
holding something down by applying pressure against counter-
pressure. Imagine a giant spring that you try with all your might
to push down, knowing that if you let go it will spring back to
its original position. So it is with traumatic experiences. Even
though we bury them, they resurface through other avenues of
our consciousness, such as dreams or repetitive gestures. One
way or another, traumatic memories always return. In the same
way, Paul writes in his Romans letter, there is a psychology to
atheism. What we fear more than nature, or more than a meaningless existence, is coming face-to-face with an almighty God
who will hold us accountable for everything we have ever done
(cf. Job 19:29; Eccles. 12:14; Matt. 12:36; Rom. 2:16; 14:10,
12; 1 Cor. 4:5). We know that our unrighteousness will become
radically exposed the moment we step into the light. God's holiness is incomprehensible. Even the angels, who are morally pure,
worship God's holiness. We humans cannot begin to fathom his
moral perfection, much less his metaphysical perfection. Seeing
God's face would send us to the grave. For this reason, we have
a natural disposition and vested interest in fleeing or repressing
the truth of God's Word. Until we submit to the authority of the
living God, we are all, like Adam and Eve, hiding in the bushes,
naked and ashamed.

We cannot bear the exposure of this nakedness. We cannot
stand the light of God's revelation. Our milieu of comfort is dark-

ness. We prefer the darkness because it conceals our wickedness. So, by nature, we suppress the light of God's revelation. We do so because we deem it necessary to protect ourselves from the pain of exposure.

But of course, this "theory" of the psychology of atheism rests upon observations from the biblical revelation. It begs the question we must now attempt to answer: Why should we trust the teachings of the Bible?

SECTION VI

The Case for
Biblical Authority

20

THE AUTHORITY OF
THE BIBLE

Some believe that the best way to do apologetics is to begin by establishing the authority of the Bible. Once that is accomplished, everything else falls in place, including the existence of God. This is not the classical strategy, however, because a defense of Scripture rests on the prior establishing of God's existence, which has been our approach in this book. Having explored questions concerning the existence of God, however, it is now time to explore the reliability of Scripture as the source of much of our information about God. As Calvin wrote, "Credibility of doctrine is not established until we are persuaded beyond doubt that God is its Author."[1] Does the Bible, in fact, persuade us beyond doubt that God is its Author?

Does the Bible Authenticate Itself?

Biblical apologists sometimes argue that the Bible is self-authenticating and therefore needs no further defense. The idea is that if the Bible is the divinely inspired Word of God, it can be subjected to no higher court of appeal outside of itself. If the Bible is divinely inspired, then it carries its own intrinsic authority and cannot be tested against anything at all, simply because there is no higher authority than God himself. If we attempt to defend the

truth claims of the Bible by using logical or empirical arguments
we risk being viewed as compromising the purity of the Christian
faith by subjecting God to human tests. This is not our intent. It is
one thing to use God's gift of reasonable thinking in apologetics;
it is quite another to presume that our reasonable thinking is the
ultimate standard of truth.

The reasoning of such an argument is clearly circular, and in
logical analysis that means the argument is fallacious. Consider
the following example: "The Bible is the Word of God. The Bible,
being the Word of God, declares that it is the Word of God.
Therefore, the Bible is the Word of God." In this syllogism, the
conclusion is already present in the premises, and so it violates
basic logic. It commits the fallacy of circular reasoning or question begging. A nonbeliever can spot this fallacy at once. It gives
the unbeliever an "excuse" for rejecting the argument.

There is yet another problem with this sort of self-authentication: the Bible is not the only book in history that claims to
be divinely inspired. Both the Qur'an and the Book of Mormon
claim the same authority as the Bible. Since there are other books
that claim to be a word from God, and since we as Christians recognize that those claims are false, we therefore also understand
that the mere fact that a writing *maintains* divine inspiration does
not make it so. There must be some criteria upon which we can
test these truth claims. This is exactly where apologetics comes
into play. By substantiating the truth claims of God's Word, we
will, in the process, distinguish the Bible's authenticity from the
spurious claims of other "holy" books.

We must be careful at this point to distinguish between at
least two distinct types of self-authentication. The first is the sort
we are rejecting, namely the idea that the Bible is the Word of
God simply because it claims to be. This would be manifest nonsense unless we could demonstrate the premise that all books that
claim to be the Word of God are in fact the Word of God.

But apologists who claim self-authentication do not mean
anything so crass as this. The argument from self-authentication

is more complex and sophisticated. If we assume for a moment that the Bible is indeed the Word of God, would it not carry the weight of its own authority?

A popular slogan on car bumpers declares, "God said it. I believe it. That settles it!" The flaw in this slogan is in the middle statement. "I believe it" implies that the truth of a matter is not settled until or unless I believe it. Rather the slogan should read, "God said it . . . that settles it!" If the Almighty opens his holy mouth, there is no room to debate with him.

But the question remains: How can we know that the words of the Bible are the veritable Word of God?

One way in which the Bible substantiates its own authority is its amazing coherency and symmetry. Its consistency over centuries and through the pens of multiple authors is nothing less than astonishing. The record of fulfilled prophecy simply between the Testaments should be evidence enough to convince the most hardened skeptic.

What the Westminster Confession called the "Heavenliness of the Matter"[2] is another indication of the Bible's divine character. The sheer transcendent majesty of the scope of Scripture leaves one breathless. No other written document in human history is worthy of comparison.

Its inner "ring of truth" gives further attestation to its authority. At a visceral level I cannot deny how acutely the Scriptures criticize my own human character flaws and corruption. The Bible pierces my soul with its moral criticism. It criticizes *me* far more effectively than I can hope to criticize *it*.

External Authentication of Scripture

These and other internal indicators serve to authenticate the Bible's claim to its own authority. In themselves they should be sufficient to stop the mouth of the skeptic. Yet if one wants *external* corroboration then we are surely able to give it. Such external corroboration includes the findings of secular historians and of archeologists.

Within the Bible itself, God himself at various times gave external proof and evidence that the word spoken had come from him. He did this not by subjecting himself to a higher test of rationality (for indeed, none exists), but by means of *miracles*. Miracles authenticate by giving outward credentials, as it were, to those who claimed to be speaking the word of God. Consider Moses and the burning bush, where the future mediator of the Old Covenant anticipated rejection from his compatriots: "But behold, they will not believe me or listen to my voice, for they will say, 'The LORD did not appear to you'" (Ex. 4:1). How did God respond? By changing Moses' staff into a serpent, and making his hand leprous (vv. 2-7). If that would not work, then God would show the people a more wondrous miracle: changing water into blood (vv. 8-9). And, as expected, the purpose of those miracles was indeed fulfilled: "Aaron spoke all the words that the LORD had spoken to Moses and did the signs in the sight of the people. And the people believed" (Ex. 4:30-31a; cf. John 10:37-38; 15:24).

We are not suggesting that one can argue from the miracle reports of the Bible to the existence of God. Before an action can be deemed a miracle or an event that only God could cause, the existence of a God capable of such action would have to be established. But the existence of just such an omnipotent, miracle-working God is precisely what we have sought to establish throughout the first five sections of this book. Readers who have followed our argument for God's existence should be prepared, when confronted with the biblical miracle stories, to agree with Nicodemus as we saw him say (in chapter 3), "Rabbi, we know that you are a teacher come from God, for no one can do these signs that you do unless God is with him" (John 3:2).

What the Bible's Authors Say About Its Authority

The various authors of the Bible either assume or explicitly claim that the words therein are inspired by Almighty God. This ratchets up the stakes of our apologetic task. Given that the central tenets of the Christian religion are unabashedly supernatural, the reliability and authority of Scripture become an even greater concern. Take, for example, the Incarnation. That Eternal God should take upon himself a human nature without setting aside his deity is an astonishing assertion. That Christ could be sinless, make a perfect atonement, be raised from the dead, and ascend into heaven are all articles of faith that would be virtually unbelievable were they not communicated in a source of impeccable authority. The Bible views the execution of Jesus not simply as the death of a criminal outside the walls of Jerusalem at the hands of the Romans. Instead it makes the radical claim that this event had cosmic significance, that it was an atonement designed before the foundations of the world to reconcile fallen creatures to a just and holy God. These supernatural occurrences inform the message throughout the New Testament, and its authors claim to be giving this message on nothing less than the authority of God himself. If they made no such claim, then it would not be necessary for us to defend the idea that the sacred Scriptures are indeed the very Word of God. But because the claim is made, it must be taken seriously.

Suppose that the Bible was not inspired. Does that automatically mean that the stories therein are false? Of course not. Reporters can get some things basically right. Eyewitnesses of Jesus, for example, could record the events with respectable accuracy. They could even assert that Jesus died as an atonement for sins, having witnessed his resurrection. We are not required to have an inspired writing for these events to be true. But given the astonishing nature of these events, *not* having an inspired witness would greatly undermine the veracity of the various testimonies.

Many stories in the Bible describe supernatural events. How are they believed? In faith, to be sure. How, then, are they defended? In faith? Not entirely. We have been arguing from the beginning that just because the Bible makes the claim of divine inspiration does not make it so. But when it makes the claim, that claim is either justified or not. If the Bible is inspired, we would expect, indeed demand, that it make good on every one of its claims. It claims, for example, that God can speak no lie (Titus 1:2); he will always remain loyal to his covenant, "for he cannot deny himself" (2 Tim. 2:13). He is no mere man who lies or changes the way he is (Num. 23:19). Secondly, the Bible claims that the Almighty Creator knows everything there is to know; he is ignorant of nothing, because he sees everything (Ps. 33:13-15; Heb. 4:13). Thirdly (and we will return to this momentarily), the Bible claims that the very words of Scripture have been "breathed out" by God himself (2 Tim. 3:16). Finally, if the above three points are accurate, then we can rightly assert that whatever claim the Bible makes must be true.

In one of his last letters to Timothy, Paul gives the young pastor admonitions and exhortations about a coming peril within the church:

> You, however, have followed my teaching, my conduct, my aim in life, my faith, my patience, my love, my steadfastness, my persecutions and sufferings that happened to me at Antioch, at Iconium, and at Lystra—which persecutions I endured; yet from them all the Lord rescued me. Indeed, all who desire to live a godly life in Christ Jesus will be persecuted, while evil people and impostors will go on from bad to worse, deceiving and being deceived. But as for you, continue in what you have learned and have firmly believed, knowing from whom you learned it . . . (2 Tim. 3:10-14).

Most of this text is easy to follow, but notice that when he tells Timothy to stay the course and endure in the direction that he has begun, Paul is basically exhorting Timothy to *remember the source of his instruction.* We can reflect on those times in our own lives when we are at the wrong end of some vicious criticism, and someone close to us, in an attempt to ameliorate our pain, says, "Consider the source," meaning, in effect, that whoever made the criticism is an unreliable source because their character cannot be taken seriously. In like manner, Paul encourages Timothy to "consider the source" of his faith in Christ. But who or what was the source? The apostle Paul? Or Timothy's mother? (see

2 Tim. 1:5). No, it was none other than the Holy Scriptures: "
. . . continue in what you have learned and have firmly believed,
knowing from whom you learned it *and how from childhood you
have been acquainted with the sacred writings,* which are able
to make you wise for salvation through faith in Christ Jesus"
(vv. 14-15, emphasis added). Then the apostle goes on, making
a spectacular claim as to the origins of these "sacred writings":
"All Scripture is *breathed out* by God and profitable for teaching, for reproof, for correction, and for training in righteousness,
that the man of God may be competent, equipped for every good
work" (vv. 16-17, emphasis added). Paul in this passage is leav-
ing no room for the idea that only parts of Scripture are inspired
by God; rather, whatever he designates by the word "Scripture"
is, in its entirety, breathed out by God. The Greek word (translated "Scripture") that Paul uses here is *graphe,* which literally
means "writing" or "a thing written." This word in first-century
Judaism often referred to what we now call the Old Testament,
and given the context of this passage, we can be assured that at
the very minimum Paul was claiming divine inspiration for all the
books before the Gospel of Matthew in our English Bibles.

The big question for us as we attempt to defend the authority
of the Bible is whether the books of the New Testament can also
be identified within the category of Scripture. It is not totally clear
from this passage that Paul had his own writings (and those of
his contemporaries) in mind. But consider 2 Peter 3:14-18, where
Peter writes:

> Therefore, beloved, since you are waiting for these [a new
> heaven and earth], be diligent to be found by him without spot
> or blemish, and at peace. And count the patience of our Lord
> as salvation, just as our beloved brother Paul also wrote to you
> according to the wisdom given him, as he does in all his letters
> when he speaks in them of these matters. There are some things
> in them that are hard to understand, which the ignorant and
> unstable twist to their own destruction, as they do the other
> Scriptures. You therefore, beloved, knowing this beforehand,

> take care that you are not carried away with the error of lawless
> people and lose your own stability. But grow in the grace and
> knowledge of our Lord and Savior Jesus Christ. To him be the
> glory both now and to the day of eternity. Amen.

Peter is obviously aware of at least a few of Paul's writings. And
he clearly understands which category Paul's writings belong to:
they belong to the *graphe,* or Scriptures. This indicates nothing
less than one apostle's judgment that the writings of the apostle
Paul are on equal ground with the God-breathed books of the
Old Testament. What is more, the one thing that keeps believers
from being "carried away with the error of lawless people" (v.
17), thereby keeping them stable and growing in grace and in the
knowledge of Christ Jesus, is saturation with the Scriptures, of
which the apostle Paul's writings are assumed to be a part. There
are other passages in the New Testament that lead to the same
conclusion, but this text is one of the most clear.

Looking briefly again at Paul's second letter to Timothy,
we must take notice of the word Paul uses to describe the
inspiration of the Scriptures—*theopneustos* or "God-breathed"
(2 Tim. 3:16). We have already referred to its actual meaning:
that the words of Scripture have been breathed out or exhaled
by God. The point here is not so much *how* God superintended
the project of writing holy books but *from whom* the very writings have originated; clearly, according to this passage, they
originated from God. The great and almighty God, Creator
of the universe, is the *source* of these sacred writings. Granted
he used human authors. Granted those human authors retain
their own nuances and idiosyncrasies. But the spiritual father
of young Timothy exhorted him to cling fast to the Scriptures
and to remember their source: God himself has revealed himself
in the words of man. The claim Paul makes here is not so much
that the Bible is inspired ("breathed-in," by divine superintendence) but that it is "expired" ("breathed out" from God). It
is a claim of the Bible's source and therefore of the *basis* or
ground of its authority.

The Scriptures themselves assert that they carry an irrefutable and absolute authority; an authority whose source is omniscient, infallible, and completely incorruptible and holy, incapable of lying or erring, is devoid of defects. If this collection of books is truly breathed out by God himself, then we, along with Calvin, can declare that "it is beyond all controversy that men ought to receive it with reverence."[3] This means that the prophets, psalmists, and narrators of the Old and New Testaments did not speak at their own instigation, but, being moved by the Holy Spirit (2 Pet. 1:21), "only uttered what they had been commissioned from heaven to declare."[4] While we have not actually defended this thesis yet, we needed to at least make clear the *claims* of Scripture regarding its divine origin. Our attention will now focus on defending these provocative claims.

21

Jesus' Teaching About Scripture

In the early 1970s, before the International Council on Biblical Inerrancy was founded, Ligonier Ministries held a small conference that focused on the reliability and authority of the Bible. Theologians from around the country gathered to explore the radical claims of Scripture regarding its divine origin. What became quite clear as the seminars progressed, was that every scholar present grounded his confidence in the authority of Scripture on the authority of Jesus Christ. This should come as no surprise; as Christians, we affirm the Lordship of Christ. It therefore follows that we also accept his teachings about the Scriptures. At first glance this approach seems to be a form of circular reasoning. Is it not circular reasoning to declare that the Bible is God's Word on the basis of the sayings of Jesus, when the only way we know that Jesus taught such things is that his teachings are found in the Bible? It might look like this on the surface, but under closer scrutiny we will see that the argument is not circular, but *linear*. What we are attempting to validate (the divine origin of the Bible) is not assumed in our argument's premise. All we need to do to begin with is recognize that at the very least the narratives of the Bible are basically reliable historical documents. Regardless of whether the Bible is divinely inspired, its content depends on a certain level of historical accuracy. Several testimonies from a widely diverse group of people are recorded on its pages. Many of those testimonies refer to Jesus and claim to be confirmed by eyewitnesses. The reader, then, is forced to decide: was Jesus who he said he was (i.e., the Son of God)? But before we answer that question, we must first show how the authority of Christ Jesus and the authority of the Bible are related.

Is the Bible Reliable?

I once ran into an old college friend while on a business trip. During our undergraduate years, we had spent much time together exploring the Bible and discussing many of its passages. Both of us were unabashedly Christian, and prayed together regularly. During our recent meeting, my friend informed me that he no longer believed that the Bible is the inspired Word of God. He was quick to add, however, that he still believed Jesus Christ is his Savior and Lord. I asked the obvious question: "How does Jesus exercise his lordship over you, if not through the words of sacred Scripture?" After all, a "lord" is someone who has authority over others, and to whom service and obedience are due. Where else than in the Bible can we find the marching orders from that Lord? From the church? If so, which church? The main problem with my friend's position was that both of his feet were firmly planted in mid-air. He wanted to maintain his conviction that Jesus is the Son of God while denying the primary source in which this information is found. Herein lies the relationship between the authority of Christ and the authority of the Bible: we cannot have knowledge about Jesus without the Bible, nor can we sustain our convictions about who he is without the Bible. The Word of God and the Word made flesh are inextricably tied together. Many Christians suffer from the same tension as my old college friend—trusting to some degree what the Bible teaches about Jesus yet maintaining a skepticism about this same Jesus' affirmation of the Bible.

Returning again to our small seminar in the early 1970s, the scholars started their defense of Scripture with the premise that the Bible is a basically trustworthy historical document—not necessarily an inspired, infallible, or inerrant document—only that it is essentially reliable, like a host of other ancient historical documents (e.g., the works of Herodotus, Josephus, Suetonius, Pliny, and Tacitus). The findings of archaeology are constantly confirming the basic historical reliability of the Scriptures. Much writing has centered on this topic. For example, F. F. Bruce's book, *The New Testament Documents: Are They Reliable?*[1] reviews clearly the evidence for a first-century dating of the New Testament books and for their historical trustworthiness. This basic reliability is what must be established first. Obviously if this premise is false then attaching any great importance to the Jesus of the Bible is an exercise in sheer credulity.

This first point will be the largest obstacle for nonbelievers. To defend the inspiration of the Bible to professing Christians is one problem; to defend it to unbelievers is another. If the "believer" claims faith in Jesus while denying that the Bible is at least *basically* reliable, their faith is exposed as empty.

Is Jesus Reliable?

If the unbeliever can be convinced that the Bible is as generally reliable as are other historical sources, then the next step is to see what this historical testimony yields concerning the character of Jesus. The question of historical reliability is so important to the defense of the Bible and its truth claims that it must be taken up first. If the Scriptures are basically unreliable, then there would be no reason to attach any significance to Jesus of Nazareth. The initial burden is quite obviously to prove not divine inspiration but simply historical reliability. On the other hand, if we are to defend the veracity of Scripture within the church, the matter can be pressed differently. We can challenge Christian critics who argue that the Bible is not basically trustworthy by asking them on what rational foundations their profession of faith rests. Did belief in Christ just pop into their minds? Of course not. They simply wish, as the tired cliché points out, "to have their cake and eat it, too." They want to have respect in the world by denying some of the more "embarrassing" aspects of Christian orthodoxy while preserving the blessings included in being a part of the Christian community.

When dealing with the question of historical reliability, there are certain rules of historiography that scholars follow in order to surmise the level of credibility of the documents in question. Such evaluations rely, of course, on empirical investigation. Each historian mentioned above (Herodotus, et al.) has been subjected to such criteria, and some of them have been found wanting on various points. Obviously, empirical research can only go so far. It can verify or falsify historical data but cannot confirm or deny supernatural events such as the appearance of angels, unless a set of petrified angel's wings were unearthed somewhere.

The postmodern perspective and methodology is at the outset already skeptical of anything supernatural. In fact, a supernatural occurrence cannot be verified or falsified, according to current standards, which consider miracles as violations of nature. Such standards do not even allow for the possibility of such an occurrence. Nevertheless, there are a host of names, places, and events within the narratives of Scripture that are open to historical verification or falsification. Once again, there has been much writing on this subject, as well as many modern testimonies from scholars who attempted to disprove the historical facts of Scripture and ended up being convicted and converted through the accuracy and reliability of such biblical writers as Luke (who has been deemed, even in some non-Christian circles, the most accurate historian of antiquity). At no time in church history has the historical reliability of the Old and New Testaments been as well-documented as it is today. Indeed, it seems that every time a lump of dirt turns over in Palestine, a new detail of biblical history receives verification. Yet, as the basic reliability of the biblical record has been verified time and again with the archaeological shovel and spade, many scholars persist in completely ignoring the data (as W. F. Albright once complained) because the findings conflict with their preconceived antipathies toward the entire concept that God spoke through the words of man.

What Did Jesus Say About the Bible?

We cannot jump instantly from historical reliability to divine inspiration, but the first premise is a necessary step for our argument to avoid a circularity that no thinking non-Christian would entertain. Our next step, once we have established the basic trustworthiness of the Bible, is to make a reasonable judgment about the person Jesus. In the pages of Scripture, Jesus claims nothing less than deity. But for the sake of argument, let us assume he merely claims to be a prophet, since most other religions of the world grant that about Jesus. If Jesus was a prophet, was he a false prophet or a true prophet? In the gospel accounts, Jesus utters prophecies not only of future events such as the destruction of Jerusalem, but of himself and his own work. If he was a true prophet, then all of his teaching must be taken seriously including his teaching concerning the Scriptures. According to Jesus, the writings of Scripture are more than generally reliable. They are the veritable words of God, unable to be broken. He not only taught that they were verbally inspired, he taught that "until heaven and earth pass away, not an iota, not a dot, will pass from the Law until all is accomplished" (Matt. 5:18; cf. Luke 16:17; 24:25-27; John 10:35; 13:18; 17:12).

To state the argument in a nutshell: first, we must show that the biblical record is historically reliable, then we must move to the biblical writers' description of Jesus' flawless character. Once that is established, we can judge his claims of prophecy to be reliable because his character is reliable, as attested by the historically reliable biblical accounts. If, then, the accuracy of his teaching is established, we can easily accept his teaching on Scripture—that it is the very Word of God.

In this progression the authority of the Bible, in its highest sense, rests upon the testimony of Jesus. The church believes the Bible to be more than basically reliable because that reliable source informs us that Jesus taught that the Bible is not merely generally reliable but is altogether reliable because it is the very Word of God.

In the face of unbelief, we must start with establishing the basic reliability of the biblical record, move on to a positive affirmation of Jesus' character, and then make the inquiry, "What did Jesus teach concerning the writings of Scripture?" In the face of negative biblical criticism within the church, however, perhaps we should phrase the question another way: "What is the Lord of the church's authoritative teaching regarding the nature of Scripture?" For in twentieth-century biblical scholarship we see an astonishing tension. We have a multitude of scholars who profess their confidence in Christ, not only as a prophet but as the veritable Son of God, who acknowledge plainly that if we know anything about the historical Jesus, we know that he accepted and taught the prevailing Jewish view of the Scriptures—namely that they were the Word of God. Yet these scholars, though they acknowledge Jesus taught that the Bible was inspired of God, say Jesus was wrong in his teaching. Not only do they teach that Jesus was wrong about Scripture but they teach that it is perfectly okay that he was wrong, because we could not reasonably expect that Jesus, in his human nature, could possibly have known that Moses didn't write the first five books of the Old Testament, which Jesus said that Moses did write. He could not be held accountable for assuming a view of Scripture that was prevalent in his day because, in his human nature, he was not omniscient. In the final analysis, the argument for the authority of Scripture within the church is reduced to a Christological argument.

These scholars agree that, from a critical perspective, it is the passages deemed "most reliable" from the Gospels that recount Jesus' view of Scripture. Few if any scholars try to argue that the historical Jesus did not embrace a high view of Scripture. Rather, that he did so is readily admitted but with the admission comes the theological justification for Jesus' being wrong about historical questions such as those relating to Moses, Abraham, and Jonah. How this squares with their profession of faith in Christ will be examined in our next chapter.

22

The Trustworthiness of the Teaching of Jesus

Those who say that Jesus was wrong in his teaching about Scripture argue that in his humanity he did not have the divine attribute of omniscience. Without omniscience, they say, there was no way he could have known that his understanding of God's Word was mistaken.

This much at least is true: to conjoin God's divine attributes with Jesus' human attributes with no distinction is a violation of historic Christian orthodoxy as expressed in the "Definition of Faith" from the Council of Chalcedon in A.D. 451. This ancient Christian document emphasized the relationship between the divine nature and the human nature in Christ Jesus:

> As to his deity, He was born from the Father before the ages, but as to his humanity, the very same one was born in the last days from the Virgin Mary, the Mother of God, for our sake and the sake of our salvation: one and the same Christ, Son, Lord, Only Begotten, acknowledged to be unconfusedly, unalterably, undividedly, inseparably in two natures, since the difference of the natures is not destroyed because of the union, but on the contrary, the character of each nature is preserved and comes together in one person and one *hypostasis* [substance], not divided or torn into two persons but one and the same Son and only-begotten God, *Logos,* Lord Jesus Christ.

The church traditionally has put a fence around the relationship of Jesus' two natures. We are outside the fence if we mix the human and the divine natures so that the divine nature "deifies" the human nature.

But Chalcedon by no means put an end to the controversy. The church has straddled the fence at different times throughout the centuries on this question of Jesus' divine and human natures. Debate on this issue has centered on Mark's record of Jesus' prophecy on the Mount of Olives about his second coming: "But concerning that day or that hour, no one knows, not even the angels in heaven, nor the Son, but only the Father" (Mark 13:32; cf. Matt. 24:36; 25:13). Surprisingly, Jesus acknowledged that he did not know when his Father would act. Responding to this difficulty, Thomas Aquinas developed what has been called the "accommodation theory." Aquinas argued that, although the divine and human natures of Jesus are in such perfect unity that whatever the divine nature knows the human nature also knows, he accommodated his human audience as he revealed things to them. While Jesus did indeed know the day and the hour of his return, for reasons undisclosed he chose not to communicate it to the disciples. The glaring problem with this theory is that it raises the question of Jesus' trustworthiness as a prophet—not to mention as a sinless Savior—by his apparent disregard for truth.

Classical Protestantism makes a clear distinction between the supernatural knowledge Jesus displayed and omniscience. Even though Jesus displayed supernatural knowledge when, for example, he met Nathanael or the woman of Sychar (John 1:46-49; 4:1-45), it does not follow that he was therefore omniscient. God is able to impart information to a person without that person's receiving the full communication of all the knowledge God has. The prophets before the coming of Christ exhibited such supernatural knowledge, yet they were not deified or considered omniscient. In like manner, Jesus predicted the destruction of Jerusalem (Matt. 24; Mark 13; Luke 21:5-36), something he could not have known in his humanity but which was revealed to him by the

Word of God. Jesus prophesied the future without destroying the limits of his humanity. God imparts *knowledge* to his prophets but not omniscience. It is one thing for the divine nature to communicate *information* to the human nature. It is quite another for the divine nature to communicate a divine *attribute* (omniscience) to the human nature. That would involve a denial of Chalcedon and a subtle form of Docetism.

Those like Karl Barth who deny the full inspiration of the Bible say rightly that Jesus was not omniscient. However they go too far by asserting that since Jesus was not all-knowing, it is acceptable that he taught error. In order for Jesus to qualify as our Savior, to gain his position as the *Agnus Dei,* the Lamb of God, the blameless sacrifice, succeeding where the first Adam failed, he must have been perfectly sinless in his humanity. Is an unknowing mistake a sin? Ignorance may excuse a sin if the ignorance could not possibly have been overcome. However, if Jesus *claimed* to know more (or less) than he actually did know, such a boast would have ethical implications.

A good teacher will not bluff if asked a question he cannot answer. He will feel morally obliged to admit ignorance on the subject rather than mislead his students with rhetorical eloquence. Jesus, however, did more than just claim to know the truth. He broke into history and declared, "For I have not spoken on my own authority, but the Father who sent me has himself given me a commandment—what to say and what to speak. . . . What I say, therefore, I say as the Father has told me" (John 12:49, 50b; cf. John 5:19; 8:28; 14:9-11). Not only does Jesus say that he bears witness to the truth (John 8:45) but he considers himself to be *the* Truth (John 14:6). And he goes even further, saying that there is another who testifies to his veracity—the Lord God omnipotent (John 5:30-47; 8:13-19). What more can be said? Jesus made as high a claim as any teacher could ever make. Given that Jesus claimed to be the veritable incarnation of truth, how could he remain sinless and still claim to know something he did not really know? Jesus spoke on many occasions about the writings of the prophets; these writings, he believed, were the sure words of God himself. He claimed to know this with certainty. He also claimed that his teachings were true, indeed, that he embodied truth. If his teaching about the Scriptures was false, then, quite frankly, he was a false teacher.

Those scholars who maintain that Jesus was mistaken about the Scriptures have so focused their attention on difficult details that they have virtually strained out a gnat and swallowed a camel (see Matt. 23:24b). They have allowed themselves to be consumed by minor problems of biblical harmony to the detriment of far weightier matters such as the integrity of Christ himself. If Jesus were wrong about anything he taught, why would we exalt him as a prophet, let alone as the Son of God? It would discredit his entire role as portrayed in the New Testament. Whether Jesus in his humanity was omniscient is not the issue; rather, it was his responsibility (in light of his sinless perfection) never to claim more authority or truth than he actually possessed. Did he lead people into the truth, or did he mislead them into error? Jesus said to the Pharisees, "If you can't believe me concerning earthly things, how can you believe me concerning heavenly things?" (see John 3:12). Sadly, we have a generation of Christian scholars who claim to believe Jesus concerning heavenly things while rejecting his teaching concerning earthly things.

Theologians like Karl Barth have argued that the doctrine of divine inspiration is nothing more than "biblical Docetism." Just as in the ancient heresies the true nature of the Son of God was compromised by those who deified the humanity of Jesus, so (these theologians would say) the doctrine of divine inspiration deifies the writers of the Bible. After all, they say, the Bible was written by humans; to suggest that the writings are infallible, then, implies that the authors themselves were divine. The Bible errs, according to Barth, simply because of its human involvement: *errare humanum est* ("to err is human"). But the Scriptures teach that its authors did not write wholly by their own instigation; rather, they were supervised by the Holy Spirit, who enabled and preserved them from their human tendency to err: "For no prophecy was ever produced by the will of man, but men spoke from God as they were carried along by the Holy Spirit" (2 Pet. 1:21).

If scholars like Barth want to make the parallel to the two natures of Christ and the Docetic heresy, we can appeal to the dual nature of God's Word. The first "nature" of Scripture is the humanity of the human authors, which includes all of the idiosyncrasies of style; the second is the deity of its ultimate author, which includes the infallible superintendence of every word, thereby elevating the book into the very word of God himself.

In the end, the burden of proof lies with those who would affirm Jesus' teachings about the heavens but deny his veracity when he spoke about things on earth. If the Bible is the Word of God only when we are reading it under the influence of the Holy Spirit, and not objectively, outside of ourselves, then all that it claims about inspiration, including Jesus' own teachings, comes crashing down, becoming nothing more than a noisy gong or a clanging cymbal.

Barth, and others, agree that the Bible is the Word of God (*Verbum Dei*), but they say that it is subject to error. Their formula may justly be summarized as follows:

The Bible is the Word of God, which errs.

This poses an insurmountable problem to the Christian. If the Bible is God's Word, it cannot err, because God cannot err. If the Bible errs, then it cannot be the Word of God. God and error . . . God and falsehood . . . can never be reconciled with each other.

23

THE TESTIMONY OF THE HOLY SPIRIT

What other evidences might there be to bolster the biblical claim that Scripture is breathed out by God? John Calvin, in his *Institutes of the Christian Religion,* offers a few interesting examples. The great Reformer undoubtedly believed that the Bible should be received with as much authority as if God himself spoke aloud for all to hear. In the *Institutes,* he gave several arguments for divine inspiration from within the pages of Scripture itself, which he believed were significant proofs. These *internal* evidences must be distinguished from external supportive arguments like those that come from the fields of science or archaeology.

Calvin's Internal Evidences for Scripture

Just after arguing that the authority of Scripture is established with certainty by being confirmed through the witness of the Holy Spirit, Calvin entered into a discussion about the "sufficiently firm proofs" that "are at hand to establish the credibility of Scripture."[1] When Calvin uses the word *proof* in this context, his Latin word is *indicia,* which we are to understand as the indicators, signs, or objective evidences that point to the credibility and by extension the supernatural origin of Scripture. These "proofs" are sufficient to make the objective case for Scripture, but lack the power to "persuade" the obstinate. They stop the mouths of the "obstreperous"[2] but do not pierce their hearts. As Calvin writes, "Unless this certainty [the confirmation by the Holy Spirit], higher and stronger than any human judgment, be present, it will be vain to fortify the authority of Scripture by arguments, to establish it by common agreement of the church, or to confirm it with other helps."[3] Before we discuss the role of the Holy Spirit in confirming Scripture, we will first explore some of the other confirmations Calvin set forth.

To begin with, Calvin gave attention to the idea that the writings in the Bible are very old. This argument from the "antiquity" of Scripture might seem unusual. We do not often hear an argument for the truthfulness of a document merely by virtue of its age. But what impressed Calvin here is not only that the books of Moses are much earlier than most other religious writings, but that what he actually wrote about concerning God was handed down age after age by the patriarchs. Given its great antiquity, the Bible has been marvelously preserved by God. It has stood the test of time. Calvin further asked the reader to ponder the care with which the Lord armed godly men to copy the Word with the utmost caution. Despite Israel's exile, wars, and almost complete extermination, "Who does not recognize as a remarkable and wonderful work of God the fact that those sacred monuments, which the wicked had persuaded themselves had utterly perished, soon returned and took their former place once more, and even with enhanced dignity?"[4] It is interesting to contemplate what Calvin might have thought about the past two hundred years of biblical criticism and the resilience of the Scriptures. The Bible has survived every assault that scholars have launched against it, and there is no reason to think that it will not continue to survive. No book ever written has been subjected to such comprehensive critical scrutiny as has the Bible.

Calvin also wrote of the heavenly character of the Scriptures, and how the Bible is far superior to all human wisdom. Not only is the Bible profoundly deep, it is transcendentally majestic, and the beauty of truth saturates every book therein. Scripture, the most erudite philosopher will find, actually scrutinizes the reader and not the other way around (Heb. 4:12). Its content is so far beyond the most creative and brilliant of insights that we stand in amazement of the sheer grandeur of its subjects. No other writing in the history of the world, Calvin argues, is capable of affecting us at all comparably to how the Scriptures affect us:

> Then, in spite of yourself, so deeply will it affect you, so pen-
> etrate your heart, so fix itself in your very marrow, that, com-
> pared with its deep impression, such vigor as the orators and
> philosophers have will nearly vanish. Consequently, it is easy to
> see that the Sacred Scriptures, which so far surpass all gifts and
> graces of human endeavor, breathe something divine.[5]

Calvin includes, in conjunction with his discussion of the majesty of Scripture, the harmony of all the portions of Scripture. Such recognition comes through the deep study of God's Word. Only then will we see the prudence of the divine wisdom, so ordered and in beautiful agreement from beginning to end. There is no other book like it—either in its morality, its justice, or its harmony. The Bible surpasses them all.

Finally, Calvin spent some time on one of the most important internal evidences, that of prophecy. When prophets like Isaiah, Jeremiah, Ezekiel, and Daniel predicted events with amazing accuracy, speculation as to the source of the prediction points in only one direction: the divine. With more than two hundred specific, detailed prophecies about the coming of the Messiah, which are recorded to have been fulfilled in Jesus, how could the inspiration of the Scriptures be denied? The answer can only be unbelief, as no amount of documentation will ever persuade the unregenerate.

The Testimony of the Holy Spirit

Calvin wrote that these and other arguments were sufficient to restrain the barking of ungodly men.[6] But he also wrote, as noted above, that people will not be duly persuaded by such objective evidence until that evidence is reinforced by the ministry and operation of the Holy Spirit.[7] On this point we must be careful or else we will fall into the same trap that those who argue from sheer fideism have fallen into: that proffering evidences to the ungodly is useless. Calvin is clearly stating that the highest proof of all for the credibility of the Scriptures is the certainty that the Holy Spirit imparts to all believers. This is, of course, outside the objective realm and into the subjective world of internal testimony and confidence. But Calvin is not retreating here to some kind of mysticism, where belief in God's Word can be attained only through a blind leap of faith. The Holy Spirit does not give the Christian new proofs in Scripture that are unavailable to everyone else. Nor does he impart new arguments or knowledge about Scripture that is unavailable to the unregenerate person. But the Spirit does enable the Christian to believe all the objective evidences we have discussed thus far. Nonbelievers can read the same Bible, grapple with the same arguments, and still lack certainty—the supernatural certainty that comes only by the supernatural ministry of the Holy Spirit. Those who do not believe, says the Bible, are at enmity with God (Rom. 8:7). They are hostile to his law, and would refuse the risen Christ even if he were standing before them. What the Holy Spirit accomplishes, then, is a breaking down of the barriers in our minds and the hostility of our hearts, thereby enabling us to surrender to the truth of God's Word. The Spirit does not move us to believe *against* the evidence but to surrender *to* the evidence that is there. The Spirit, said Calvin, causes us to "acquiesce into the *indicia.*"[8]

Because the work of the Spirit is essential for regeneration, none of our arguments for the divine origin of Scripture can be our starting place in the apologetic task. "They who strive to build up firm faith in Scripture through disputation," Calvin writes, "are doing things backwards."[9] Although we can answer the retorts of those who deny the veracity of the Bible and can "clear God's Sacred Word from man's evil speaking, [we] will not at once imprint upon their hearts that certainty which piety requires."[10] Calvin wrote not that we should give up this task, but that we should know that the Word will not find acceptance in the hearts of people before they are sealed by the inward testimony of the Holy Spirit. The first move for us, then, in this apologetic endeavor, is to present persuasive arguments for the existence of God. We want to do this in such a way that to deny God's existence would be an obvious affirmation of absurdity. We focus on those things that all people must confirm in order to maintain some semblance of sanity in their lives: the four foundations of knowledge that we considered in chapters 3-8. As we have seen, denying any one of these foundations leads to absurdity, while following them to their ultimate end can only point to a rational Creator. We are all created in the image of this God; at the very least we have that in common with the unregenerate person. For this reason, the starting point in our apologetic task will be nothing less than exploring those commonalties—and then letting the Holy Spirit do his work.

Conclusion

As we conclude this introduction to the defense of Christianity, we inquire about the significance of what we have examined. We have looked at only two issues—the case for the existence of God and the case for the divine origin of the sacred Scriptures. The scope of the science of apologetics, of course, goes far beyond these two issues. In every generation, competing secular philosophies collide with the truth claims of Christianity.

In any worldview we are dealing with a system of thought. That system of thought may or may not be consistent and internally coherent. Most systems seek to be coherent and to speak to a wide diversity of issues. Christianity is concerned not merely about how we worship or how we pray; it is interested in the character of God. It is interested in the question of cosmology—that is, how this world is constructed. Does this world operate by internal fixed laws that are independent from the power of God, or does nature itself depend every moment for its power and operations upon this transcendent God who created it in the first place? There are issues of anthropology: are we, as human beings, created in the image of God for a purpose and therefore our lives have meaning and significance; or are we grown-up germs, cosmic accidents, who have no significance in the final analysis? How we understand God determines how we understand the world; and how we understand God and the world determines how we understand our place within the grand scheme of things.

Christianity as a worldview is always in competition with and on a collision course with alternate systems of thought. Today's apologists might have to duel with the existentialists or the analytical philosophers where in the past other philosophies were encountered. Whatever will be in vogue tomorrow will provoke new questions, new issues, and new responses from the Christian community.

One of the things we enjoy as Christians, having had two thousand years of practice in dealing with alternate systems, is that when we are confronted by a new philosophical challenge to the Christian faith, where we have to defend ourselves afresh in a new generation, we have the advantage of two thousand years of reflection on issues that tend to come up over and over again. One of the problems new philosophies encounter is that they don't have that backlog of resources concerning their points of vulnerability. That gives them an advantage as they come on the scene: nobody has thought about the points of vulnerability that they might have. But when they are exposed to the second glance of philosophical scrutiny, they tend to have a short life span. Alternate philosophies come and go through church history while orthodox Christianity remains.

Historically, the great theologians and apologists of church history have agreed that all truth is one and that all truth meets at the top. What God reveals in Scripture will not contradict what he reveals to us outside of Scripture in the realm of nature. Conversely, if God reveals some truth in nature, that truth will not contradict what is found in the Bible.

When we establish the two premises that we have examined— the existence of God and the authority of the Bible—we have gone ninety percent of the way in the task of apologetics, even though there may be ten thousand more questions we have to deal with. By establishing the existence of God and thereby the authority of Scripture, the last ten percent can be dealt with by a careful study of what Scripture says.

Far from being a threat, there is no greater liberation for the seeker of truth than the certainty that God exists and reveals himself and his will in the special revelation of sacred Scripture.

NOTES

CHAPTER 1
THE TASK OF APOLOGETICS

1. John Calvin, *Institutes of the Christian Religion*, ed. John T. McNeill, trans. Ford Lewis Battles, vol. 20 of The Library of Christian Classics (Philadelphia: Westminster, 1960), I.8.8 (88).
2. John Calvin, *Institutes of the Christian Religion*, ed. Henry Beveridge, vol. 1 (Grand Rapids, Mich.: Eerdmans, 1962), I.7.4 (71).

CHAPTER 4
THE LAW OF NONCONTRADICTION

1. Allan Bloom, *The Closing of the American Mind* (New York: Simon & Schuster, 1987), 25-26.
2. Aristotle *Metaphysics*, IV.3.8.

CHAPTER 6
THE LAW OF CAUSALITY

1. John Stuart Mill, *Three Essays on Religion* (New York: Henry Holt, n.d.), 147.
2. John Stuart Mill, quoted in Bertrand Russell, *Why I Am Not a Christian, and Other Essays on Religion and Related Subjects* (London: G. Allen & Unwin, 1957), 4.
3. Russell, *Why I Am Not a Christian*, 3-4.

CHAPTER 7
HUME'S CRITIQUE OF CAUSALITY AND THE
BASIC RELIABILITY OF SENSE PERCEPTION

1. David Hume, *An Enquiry Concerning Human Understanding / A Letter from a Gentleman to His Friend in Edinburgh*, ed. Eric Steinberg (Indianapolis: Hackett, 1977), 18.

CHAPTER 9
NATURAL THEOLOGY AND SCIENCE

1. See John Calvin, *Institutes of the Christian Religion*, ed. John T. McNeill, trans. Ford Lewis Battles, vol. 20 of The Library of Christian Classics (Philadelphia: Westminster, 1960), I.3.1 (43-44).
2. Widely attributed to Galileo Galilei, who may have been quoting Cardinal Cesare Baronius.

3. Thomas Aquinas, *Nature and Grace: Selections from the Summa Theologica of Thomas Aquinas,* trans. and ed. A. M. Fairweather, vol. 11 of The Library of Christian Classics (Philadelphia: Westminster, 1954), 137.

CHAPTER 10
AQUINAS AND KANT

1. See *Saint Anselm, Basic Writings,* trans. S. N. Deane, with an introduction by Charles Hartshorne, 2nd edn. (LaSalle, Ill.: Open Court, 1968).
2. Immanuel Kant, *Prolegomena to Any Future Metaphysics,* ed. Paul Carus (Chicago: Open Court, 1949), 7.
3. Norman Geisler, *Baker Encyclopedia of Christian Apologetics* (Grand Rapids, Mich: Baker, 1999), 402.
4. Fyodor Dostoevsky, *The Brothers Karamazov* (New York: Norton, 1976), 72.

CHAPTER 12
SELF-CREATION

1. R. C. Sproul, *Not a Chance: The Myth of Chance in Modern Science and Cosmology* (Grand Rapids, Mich: Baker, 1994).

CHAPTER 16
THE GOD OF THE PHILOSOPHERS AND THE GOD OF THE BIBLE

1. Antony Flew, "Theology and Falsification," 1950, reprinted in *Philosophy Now* 29 (October/ November 2000): 28-29.

CHAPTER 18
THE NIHILISTS

1. Jean-Paul Sartre, *Being and Nothingness,* trans. with introduction by Hazel E. Barnes (New York: Philosophical Library, 1956), 615.

CHAPTER 19
THE PSYCHOLOGY OF ATHEISM

1. Sigmund Freud, *Civilization and Its Discontents,* trans. and ed. James Strachey (New York: W. W. Norton, 1961), 19.

CHAPTER 20
THE AUTHORITY OF THE BIBLE

1. John Calvin, *Institutes of the Christian Religion,* ed. John T. McNeill, trans. Ford Lewis Battles, vol. 20 of The Library of Christian Classics (Philadelphia: Westminster, 1960), I.7.4 (78).
2. *The Westminster Confession of Faith,* I.5.

3. John Calvin, *Commentaries on the Epistles to Timothy, Titus, and Philemon,* trans. William Pringle (Grand Rapids, Mich.: Eerdmans, 1948), 248.

4. Ibid.

CHAPTER 21
JESUS' TEACHING ABOUT SCRIPTURE

1. F. F. Bruce, *The New Testament Documents: Are They Reliable?* (Downers Grove, Ill.: InterVarsity, 1960).

CHAPTER 23
THE TESTIMONY OF THE HOLY SPIRIT

1. John Calvin, *Institutes of the Christian Religion,* ed. John T. McNeill, trans. Ford Lewis Battles, vol. 20 of The Library of Christian Classics (Philadelphia: Westminster, 1960), I.7-8 (74-92).

2. John Calvin, *Institutes of the Christian Religion,* ed. Henry Beveridge, vol. 1 (Grand Rapids, Mich.: Eerdmans, 1962), I.7.4 (71).

3. John Calvin, *Institutes,* ed. McNeill, I.8.1 (81).

4. Ibid., I.8.10 (90).

5. Ibid., I.8.1 (82).

6. Ibid., I.8.8 (88).

7. Ibid., I.7.4-5; I.8.1 (78-83).

8. Ibid., I.7.5 (80).

9. Ibid., I.7.4 (78).

10. Ibid.

General Index

Scripture Index